FABULOUS
FINGER FOODS

BELLE SCULLY
Celebrity Chefs' Cookbooks

FABULOUS
FINGER
FOODS

Times Editions

The publisher wishes to thank
Living Quarters Sdn Bhd, Malaysia for the loan and use of their tableware.

Chef: Belle Scully
Managing Editor: Jamilah Mohd Hassan
Editor of the English Edition: Yeo Puay Khoon
Art Direction: Christopher Wong
Designer: Tan Shiang Chin
Photographer: Suan I. Lim
Project Co-ordinator: Christine Chong
Production Co-ordinator: Nor Sidah Haron

© 2004 Marshall Cavendish International (Asia) Private Limited

Published by Times Editions — Marshall Cavendish
An imprint of Marshall Cavendish International (Asia) Private Limited
A member of the Times Publishing Limited
Times Centre, 1 New Industrial Road, Singapore 536196
Tel: (65) 6213 9288   Fax: (65) 6285 4871
E-mail: te@sg.marshallcavendish.com
Online Bookstore: http://www.timesone.com.sg/te

Malaysian Office:
Federal Publications Sdn Berhad
(General & Reference Publishing) (3024-D)
Times Subang, Lot 46, Persiaran Teknologi Subang
Subang Hi-Tech Industrial Park
Batu Tiga, 40000 Shah Alam
Selangor Darul Ehsan, Malaysia
Tel: (603) 5635 2191   Fax: (603) 5635 2706
E-mail: cchong@tpg.com.my

All rights reserved. No part of this publication may be reproduced,
stored in a retrieval system or transmitted, in any form or by any means,
electronic, mechanical, photocopying, recording or otherwise,
without the prior permission of the copyright owner.

National Library Board (Singapore) Cataloguing in Publication Data

Scully, Belle.
Fabulous finger foods / Belle Scully. – Singapore : Times Editions, c2004.
p. cm. – (Celebrity chefs' cookbooks)
ISBN : 981-232-406-2

1. Appetizers. 2. Snack foods. I. Title. II. Series: Celebrity chefs' cookbooks

TX740
641.812 – dc21   SLS2004008509

Printed in Singapore by Times Printers Pte Ltd

My sincere thanks to my husband, Terrence, my son, Jonathan and daughter Sonia Dawn for encouraging and helping me to get this book going. A big thank you to my family members, friends and culinary associates. My sincere appreciation and thanks to Marshall Cavendish for giving me this opportunity.

CONTENTS

Preface 8 **Glossary 80** **Weights & Measures 84**

Mixed Fruit Meringues	10	Custard Prawn Fritters	28
Cheese Straws	10	Platter of Peanut Crackers and Dips	29
Pepperoni Topped Potatoes	12	Malaysian Peanut Butter & Corn Pancakes	30
Mini Burgers	12	Fried Mozzarella in Couscous	30
Mini Pizzas	14	Chipolata with Cheese and Ham Wraps	32
Spicy Honey Drumlets	14	Avocado Anchovy Dip on Crackers	33
Vol-au-vents	16	BBQ Hot and Spicy Prawns	34
Mince Pies	16	Pinwheel Cheese and Walnut Sandwiches	34
Fruit Agar-agar	18	Viennese Almond Crescents	36
Chicken Drumlets	19	Mexican Nachos	37
Salmon Finger Sandwiches	20	Brandy Snaps	38
Fried Bean Curd with Peanut Sauce	20	Mini Herb and Garlic Sandwiches	39
Hot Garlic Cheese Puffs	22	Grilled Orange Chicken Bites	40
Coconut Church Candy	22	Cheese Almond Fingers	40
Fried Crispy Wantons	24	Apple Walnut Muffins	42
Curried Egg and Cucumber Sandwiches	24	Curry Puffs	42
Chocolate-dipped Shortbread Fingers	26	Spiced Lamb Kofta	44
Mint Tomatoes	26	Coconut Squares	45

Mini Popiahs	46	Superb Salmon Dip	64
Cherry Nut Biscuits	46	Tiramisu Cream Profiteroles	64
Barbecued Chicken Skewers	48	Beef, Asparagus and Capsicum Rolls	66
Tropical Coconut Prawns with Mango Sauce	49	Savoury Pepperoni Squares	66
Blueberry Cheese Tartlets	50	Japanese Bean Curd with Sambal Prawns	68
Lamb Meatballs with Creamy Mint Sauce	50	Almond Petit Fours	69
Palmiers with Cucumber Dip	52	Turkey Fruit Sticks	70
Mini Cold Cuts and Seafood Terrines	52	Fruity Kebabs	70
Savoury Masala Nuts	54	Wicked Brownies	72
Almond Prawn Toast	54	Prawn Egg Rolls	73
Vegetable Tempura with Mustard Dip	56	Tomato Cheese Tartlets	74
Filled Top Hats/Pie Tee Shells	56	Olive and Smoked Turkey Squares	74
Sardine Cones	58	Spicy Herb Potato Wedges	76
Thai Fish Cakes with Chilli Dip	59	Spicy Chicken Nibbles	76
Bruschetta with Toppings	60	A Tray of Truffles	78
Egg Rosettes	60	Cucumber Slices with Cheese Topping	79
Crab Claws	62		
Seafood Nibbles with Chilli Dip	62		

PREFACE

Like most cooks, when I learnt cooking in my parents' kitchen, I burnt a lot of food—good food! But encouragement from my dad, who was the 'chef' in our home and my mom, who was his assistant, spurred me on.

The rest is history and today I am here with my *Fabulous Finger Foods* book with a little something for everyone. It is not a book of specialised recipes, but rather it allows you to explore a world of flavours. Feel free to improvise on these recipes using the ingredients that you prefer. I stand in awe of God's creations and the talent and skills He blesses us with.

Belle Scully

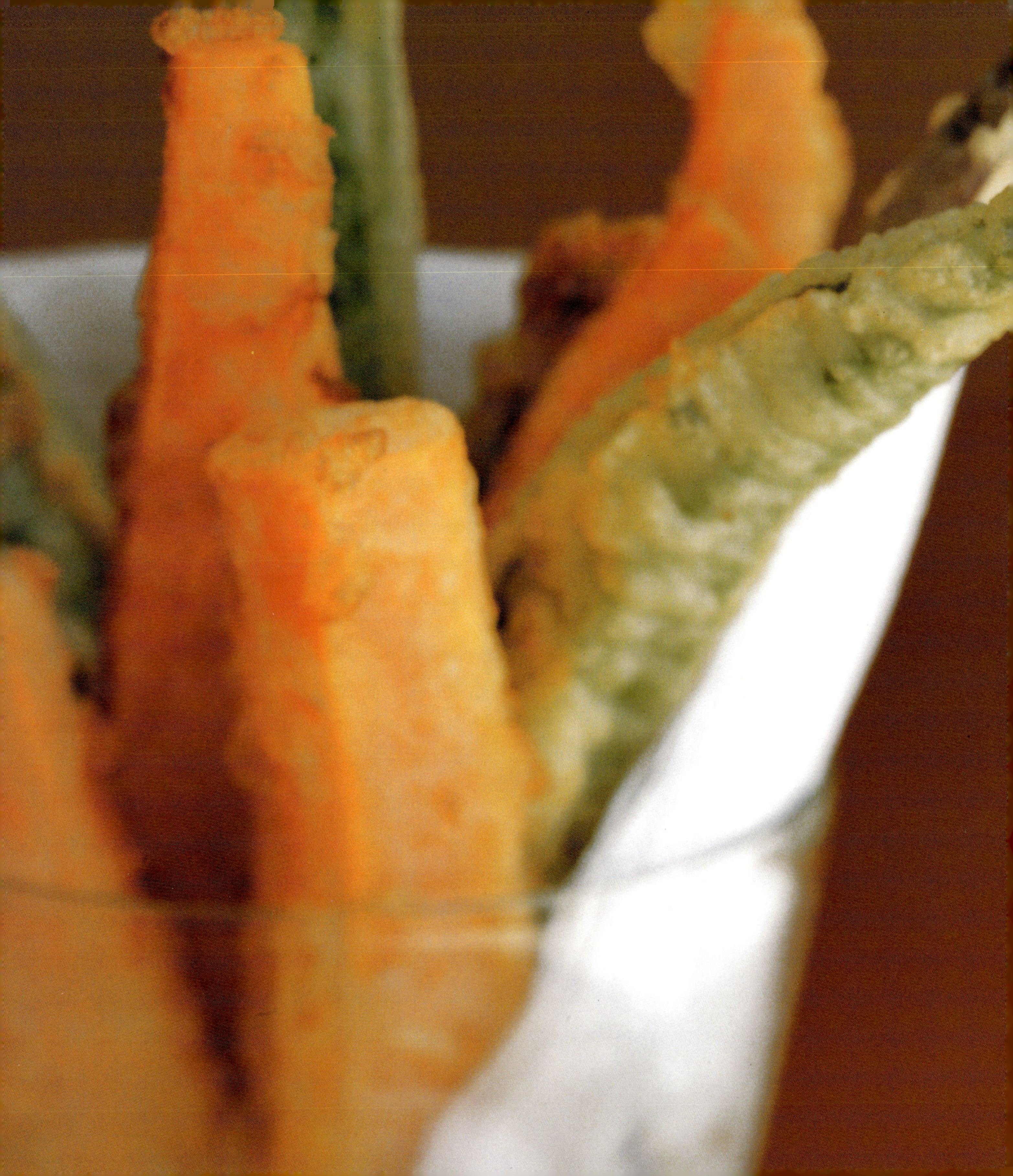

Preparation time: 30 minutes   Cooking time: 15 minutes   Serves 6–8

MIXED FRUIT MERINGUES

INGREDIENTS

Butter for greasing	
Cornflour (cornstarch)	½ tsp

MERINGUE

Egg	1, white only
Cold water	2 Tbsp
Castor sugar	120 g
Vanilla essence	½ tsp
Vinegar	1 tsp

COINTREAU FILLING

Whipping cream	300 ml
Cointreau liqueur	1 Tbsp, optional
Strawberries	5–6
Kiwi fruit	1, skinned and sliced
Fresh cherries	5–6
Mango	1, skinned and sliced

COINTREAU AND APRICOT GLAZE

Apricot jam	1 Tbsp
Cointreau liqueur	1 Tbsp
Water	1 Tbsp

METHOD

- Grease 2 baking trays with butter. Dust with cornflour and shake off excess.
- Mark 10 rounds, each measuring 4-cm in diameter, on each tray.
- Combine meringue ingredients in a mixing bowl.
- Beat on high speed for about 15 minutes, until mixture is thick and sugar is completely dissolved.
- Transfer the meringue mixture to a large piping bag with a 5-mm plain tube nozzle.
- Pipe meringue cases by starting in the middle of a marked round, piping a concentric circle, so that the circle is covered with meringue. Continue piping, without stopping, to build up sides of meringue cases. Pipe about four layers.
- Place in preheated oven at 170–180°C and reduce heat immediately to 150°C. Bake for 30 minutes or until dry to touch.
- Gently lift cooked cases from trays onto a wire rack to cool. Pipe whipped cream, with 1 Tbsp Cointreau liqueur added (optional), into each case and top with fresh fruits.
- Mix cointreau and apricot glaze ingredients together over a gentle heat. Glaze fruits.

Chef's Note:

- *Always transfer meringue mixture all at once into piping bag. Refilling the bag will cause air bubbles to form.*
- *Do not handle meringue mixture too much or it will deflate.*
- *Fill meringue cases 1 hour before serving.*
- *Meringue cases can also be filled with roasted almonds or crushed praline.*

Preparation time: 15 minutes   Chilling time: 10 minutes
Cooking time: 10 minutes   Serves 4–6

CHEESE STRAWS

INGREDIENTS

Butter	75 g
Plain (all-purpose) flour	150 g
Cheddar cheese	75 g, grated
Parmesan cheese	1 Tbsp, grated
Mustard powder	¼ tsp
Cayenne pepper	1 tsp
Cold water	2 Tbsp
Milk	60 ml for brushing
Poppy seeds or sesame seeds	1 tsp

SOUR CREAM DIP

Mayonnaise	4 Tbsp
Sour cream	4 Tbsp
Lemon juice	1 Tbsp
Chilli sauce	3 Tbsp
Salt and freshly ground black pepper	to taste
Green apple	1, skinned, cored and finely diced

METHOD

- Preheat oven to 180°C. Rub butter into flour until it resembles breadcrumbs.
- Stir in cheeses and spices. Add iced water and mix to form a smooth dough.
- Roll out on a floured surface into a thin 30 x 10-cm sheet.
- Cut out strips of dimensions 1 x 10-cm. Twist once or twice and place on a greased baking tray.
- Repeat with any leftover trimmings. Brush with milk and sprinkle with a few poppy or sesame seeds. Chill for 10 minutes.
- Bake for 10–20 minutes, until golden. Cool on a wire rack.
- Prepare sour cream dip. Mix mayonnaise, sour cream, lemon juice, chilli sauce, salt and pepper together until smooth. Stir in diced apple. Chill before serving with cheese straws.

Chef's Note:

- *1 tsp of chilli powder or curry powder can be added to the above recipe for spicy cheese straws.*
- *Cheese straws can be frozen and reheated at 190–200°C for 5–10 minutes until crisp.*
- *These cheese straws are extra good due to the crumbly rich pastry. It is so much easier to roll pastry between 2 sheets of greaseproof paper or plastic sheets.*

From top: Cheese Straws; Mixed Fruit Meringues

Preparation time: 5 minutes   Cooking time: 30 minutes   Serves 6–8

PEPPERONI TOPPED POTATOES

INGREDIENTS

New potatoes	12
Olive oil	1 Tbsp
Pepperoni	100 g, finely chopped
Sour cream	125 ml
Chopped spring onions (scallions)	1 Tbsp
Lemon juice	3 tsp
Shallot	1, peeled and chopped
Red chilli	1, seeded and chopped

METHOD

- Boil, steam, microwave or bake potatoes until tender; if boiled, drain and cool.
- Heat olive oil in a pan and stir-fry chopped pepperoni until crisp. Drain and cool. Reserve 1 Tbsp of pepperoni for garnishing.
- Combine sour cream, spring onions, lemon juice, shallot, red chilli and pepperoni in a bowl; mix well.
- Cut potatoes in half then cut a small slice off base of each potato. Stand potatoes on a serving plate.
- Top each potato with 1 level tsp of sour cream mixture. Sprinkle reserved pepperoni on top.

Chef's Note:

- *Potatoes can be made several hours in advance. Keep covered in refrigerator.*
- *Instead of pepperoni, salami or tuna can be used as substitutes.*
- *If desired, a little chopped pineapple can be added to the sour cream mixture.*

Preparation time: 30 minutes   Cooking time: 10 minutes   Serves 4–6

MINI BURGERS

INGREDIENTS

Bread	6 slices
Garlic butter	2 Tbsp
Tomato sauce	2 Tbsp
Grated Mozzarella cheese	½ cup

MEAT PATTIES

Olive oil	2 Tbsp
Onion	1, peeled and chopped
Garlic	2 cloves, peeled and grated
Ginger	1 tsp, peeled and grated
Minced beef	250 g
Chopped spring onions (scallions)	1 Tbsp
French mustard	1 tsp
Freshly ground black pepper	1 tsp
Balsamic vinegar	2 tsp
Salt	to taste
Cooking oil	

METHOD

- Heat oil in a non-stick pan and sauté the onion, garlic and ginger until.
- Pour oil into a mixing bowl, add in minced beef, spring onions, mustard, black pepper and Balsamic vinegar. Add a little salt and mix well.
- Shape 2 level tsp of mixture into a ball then flatten to a 3-cm patty. Repeat with remaining mixture.
- Heat oil in a pan and cook patties until brown; drain on absorbent paper.
- Using a 4-cm ring cutter, cut 4 rounds from each slice of bread.
- Brush rounds with garlic butter and toast bread in an open toaster until lightly browned and crisp.
- Spread each round with tomato ketchup then top with meat patties and cheese.
- Just before serving, grill burgers until cheese has melted.

Chef's Note:

- *Minced chicken can be used instead of minced beef.*
- *Mini burgers can be prepared overnight but spread cheese just before serving.*
- *You can use either fresh herbs or dried herbs.*

Centre: Pepperoni Topped Potatoes; Around: Mini Burgers

Preparation time: 30 minutes   Cooking time: 15 minutes   Serves 10–12

MINI PIZZAS

INGREDIENTS

Plain (all-purpose) flour	225 g
Salt	1 tsp
Sugar	1 tsp
Dry yeast	7 g
Warm water	125 ml + extra 125 ml
Olive oil	1 Tbsp
Warm milk	60 ml

TOMATO SAUCE TOPPING

Tomato paste	125 ml
Tomato sauce	60 ml
Dried oregano leaves	1 Tbsp
Olive oil	1 Tbsp

TOPPING

Capsicum (bell pepper)	1, small, cubed
Pineapple rings	2, cubed
Pepperoni	100 g, finely sliced
Grated Mozzarella cheese	60 g

METHOD

- Sift flour and salt into a bowl.
- Combine sugar, yeast and water in a bowl and stand for 7–10 minutes or until foamy.
- Stir yeast mixture, oil and enough extra water to mix to a soft dough.
- Knead dough on lightly floured surface for 10 minutes.
- Place dough in lightly oiled bowl. Cover and let it stand in a warm place for 30 minutes.
- Knead dough and divide into half.
- Roll each to 20 x 25-cm rectangles.
- Spread with tomato sauce and topping mixture on each rectangle.
- Roll up tightly from long side then cut into 1-cm slices. Place slices cut-side up on greased oven trays.
- Bake slices in a preheated oven at 180°C for 15–20 minutes.
- Meanwhile, prepare the tomato sauce topping. Combine all the ingredients in a bowl and mix well to combine.

Chef's Note:

- Always cover dough well during rising to prevent a skin forming on the surface. Use a lightly greased cling film sheet.
- Dried yeast is very convenient as it is readily available and will keep up to 6 months if stored unopened in a cool dry place.

Preparation time: 15 minutes   Cooking time: 25–30 minutes   Serves 4–6

SPICY HONEY DRUMLETS

INGREDIENTS

Chicken wings	10–12
Honey	1–2 Tbsp

MARINADE

Yoghurt	1 Tbsp
Chilli powder	1 tsp
Curry powder	2 tsp
Salt	1 tsp
Freshly ground black pepper	1 tsp
Cooking oil	2 Tbsp
Barbecue sauce	1 Tbsp

METHOD

- Cut joints from wings. Separate second and third joints. Trim around bone with sharp knife. Push meat down to large end. Using fingers, pull skin and meat over end of bone. Leave the second joints as they are.
- Place chicken in a bowl together with marinade ingredients.
- Bake chicken in a preheated oven at 170–180°C for about 20 minutes.
- When done, marinate with honey and allow to bake for a further 5 minutes. Cool then wrap exposed ends of drumlets in foil.
- Serve with a chilli dip.

Chef's Note:

- Drumlets can be marinated and refrigerated 24 hours before baking so it can be prepared a day ahead.

From top: Spicy Honey Drumlets; Mini Pizzas

Preparation time: 20 minutes   Cooking time: 15 minutes   Serves 4–6

VOL-AU-VENTS

INGREDIENTS

Puff pastry	1 packet (375 g)
Egg yolk	1, beaten
Parsley	

FILLING

Butter	120 g
Plain (all-purpose) flour	2 Tbsp
Milk	80 ml
Dry white wine	60 ml
Whipping cream	80 ml
Mayonnaise	1 Tbsp
Chopped parsley	1 Tbsp
Salt	1 tsp
Freshly ground black pepper	1 tsp
Prawns (shrimps)	500 g, seasoned with salt and pepper

METHOD

- Melt 60 g butter in a pan and add flour. Cook for a few minutes, stirring continuously.
- Remove from heat then stir in milk and blend until smooth. Stir in wine, cream and mayonnaise.
- Return to heat and stir until sauce boils and thickens. Reduce heat, continue stirring and simmer for 2 minutes. Stir in chopped parsley. Season with salt and pepper.
- Melt remaining butter in another pan and sauté prawns until done. Add prawns to the above mixture. Leave aside.
- On a lightly floured surface, roll out pastry into a 3-mm thick sheet measuring 25 x 35-cm. Cut in half.
- Using a 5.5-cm circular cutter, cut out 6 rounds on one half. Lightly brush the other half with water.
- Gently place cut out rounds onto the other half.
- Using a 7.5-cm circular cutter, cut out larger rounds around the 5.5-cm rounds.
- Lift onto lightly greased oven trays. Refrigerate overnight.
- Brush only the top rims with beaten egg yolk. Bake in a preheated oven at 200–220°C for 5 minutes then reduce heat to moderate at 170–180°C and bake for a further 15 minutes or until pastry is well browned and risen.
- Place pastry cases onto a wire rack to cool.
- Spoon in filling and garnish with parsley.

Chef's Note:

- *Refrigerating the cut out pastry overnight will help it keep its shape while baking.*
- *Brush only the top rims of pastry and not the sides or the pastry will not rise.*
- *For perfect shapes of Vol-au-vents, it is ideal to suspend a wire rack over the Vol-au-vent about 3 cm higher than the baking tray. Alternatively, prick each top four times at equal spacing with a skewer before baking; this will also ensure that the sides of the cases rise equally.*

Preparation time: 30 minutes   Cooking time: 25 minutes   Serves 8–10

MINCE PIES

INGREDIENTS

Butter	250 g
Plain (all-purpose) flour	500 g
Icing (confectioners') sugar	50 g
Almonds	50 g, finely chopped
Egg yolks	2
Iced water	4–5 Tbsp
Orange	1, rind grated and juiced
Mincemeat mixture*	500 g
Egg	1

METHOD

- Cut butter into cubes. Sift flour into a mixing bowl. Add butter and rub into flour until it resembles fine breadcrumbs. Stir in icing sugar and almonds. Make a well in the centre, stir in egg yolks, iced water, orange rind and juice. Knead lightly to form a smooth dough. Chill for 30 minutes.
- Preheat oven to 200°C. On a floured surface, roll out two-thirds of dough and cut out 30 rounds using a 6-cm fluted cutter. Use to line patty tins.
- Fill with mincemeat.
- Re-roll remaining pastry trimmings and cut out stars using star-shaped cutter. Place star shapes on pies, brush with beaten egg and bake for 25 minutes.

*MINCEMEAT MIXTURE

Granny Smith apple	1, finely chopped
Currants	80 g
Sultanas	125 g
Raisins	125 g
Gláce ginger	75 g, chopped
Gláce cherries	5 g, chopped
Mixed peel	75 g
Almonds	50 g, chopped
Brown sugar	125 g
Butter	75 g
Cloves	1 tsp
Cinnamon	1 tsp
Nutmeg	1 tsp
Allspice	½ tsp
Ground ginger	1 tsp
Orange	1, rind grated and juiced
Brandy	75 ml (optional)
Sherry	75 ml (optional)

METHOD

- Place all ingredients in a bowl. Mix well to blend. Cover and leave in a cool place for a day. Stir, and if the mixture seems dry, add a little more alcohol.
- Spoon into clean sterilized dry jars leaving a little space at the top. Seal and label, store mincemeat in a cool dry place for 2 months before using.

Chef's Note:

- *Freeze pies either baked or unbaked in patty tins. Bake from frozen in a preheated oven at 180°C for 20–25 minutes. Defrost baked pies for 2–3 hours at room temperature when required. Reheat in a hot oven for 5 minutes.*

From top: Vol-au-vents; Mince Pies

Preparation time: 10 minutes   Cooking time: 15 minutes   Serves 6–8

FRUIT AGAR-AGAR

INGREDIENTS

Water	1.25 litres
Sugar	200 g
Agar-agar powder	2 tsp
Mixed fruit cocktail or fresh fruits	1 can (565 g)
Lemon juice	1 Tbsp

METHOD
- Bring water and sugar to a near boil and add in agar-agar powder. Stir to dissolve powder.
- Turn off heat and add in fruit cocktail and lemon juice. Pour into individual moulds and allow to set.
- Allow to cool then chill.

Chef's Note:
- *Different colours and flavourings can be used instead of just plain agar-agar. Konnyaku jelly powder can also be used—just follow the instructions on the packet.*

Preparation time: 30 minutes   Cooking time: 20 minutes   Serves 4–6

CHICKEN DRUMLETS

INGREDIENTS

Chicken wings	1 kg, about 12 pieces
Salt and pepper	to taste
Prawns (shrimps)	500 g, shelled, cleaned and finely chopped
Sugar	½ tsp
Cornflour (cornstarch)	1 tsp
Light soy sauce	1 Tbsp
Eggs	2, beaten
Sesame seeds	2 Tbsp, combined with 240 g breadcrumbs
Cooking oil	500 ml for deep-frying

METHOD

- Wash and dry chicken wings. Cut off wing tips at the joint and freeze for use in other recipes.
- Holding large end of bone, cut around the bone with a sharp knife to separate meat from bone. Scrape and pull skin and meat down and over the small end of bone, forming a cavity at the top. Marinate with salt and pepper. Set aside.
- Marinate chopped prawns with sugar, cornflour, soy sauce, salt and pepper. Mix until well combined.
- Fill cavity in chicken wings with teaspoonful of prawn filling.
- Coat meat end in beaten eggs then coat with combined sesame seeds and breadcrumbs. Repeat the step to give a firm coating.
- Heat oil in a wok and gently deep-fry drumlets for about 5 minutes, until golden brown.
- Serve with soy sauce and chilli sauce.

Chef's Note:
- *These chicken drumlets can be prepared and kept in the refrigerator overnight. They can also be prepared without prawn stuffing and can either be roasted or deep-fried.*
- *When deep-frying, do not overheat oil or breadcrumbs will brown before chicken drumlets are cooked.*

Preparation time: 20 minutes   Serves 4–6

SALMON FINGER SANDWICHES

INGREDIENTS

BREAD
Unsalted butter	250 g, creamed
White bread	½ loaf (210 g)
Wholemeal bread	1 loaf (420 g)

FILLING 1
Salmon	1 can (250 g), drained
Mayonnaise	1 Tbsp
Lemon juice	1 tsp
Freshly ground black pepper	½ tsp

FILLING 2
Cucumber	1, thinly sliced
Grated lemon rind	1 tsp

METHOD
- Butter white bread on both sides and wholemeal bread on one side only.
- Combine salmon, mayonnaise, lemon juice and pepper.
- Place half of the wholemeal bread slices on a flat tray. Spread evenly with salmon mixture.
- Top with white slices. Top with cucumber and lemon rind and finish with remaining wholemeal slices.
- Using a serrated knife, trrim crusts from sandwiches. Cut each sandwich into three fingers.

Chef's Note:
- *Sandwiches are best made close to serving time. If necessary, they can be made earlier, covered with cling film and stored in the refrigerator for up to 2–3 hours.*

Preparation time: 15 minutes   Cooking time: 15 minutes   Serves 4–6

FRIED BEAN CURD WITH PEANUT SAUCE

INGREDIENTS
Cooking oil	for deep-frying
Soy bean cakes (*tauhu*)	6 pieces
Carrot	1, small, peeled and shredded
Cucumber	1, small, peeled and shredded

PEANUT SAUCE
Red chillies	3
Green chillies	3
Garlic	2 cloves
Dark soy sauce	1½ Tbsp
Vinegar	1½ Tbsp
Water	180 ml, boiled
Roasted peanuts (groundnuts)	1 cup, coarsely pounded
Salt and sugar	to taste

METHOD
- Heat oil and deep-fry bean curd until golden brown. Leave to cool. Cut each piece diagonally across into two triangular pieces.
- Make a deep slit down the centre of each piece. Stuff with shredded carrot and cucumber. Set aside.
- Prepare peanut sauce. Blend chillies with garlic. Combine all the ingredients until smooth.
- Serve stuffed fried bean curd with peanut sauce.

From left: Salmon Finger Sandwiches; Fried Bean Curd with Peanut Sauce

Preparation time: 20 minutes   Cooking time: 30–35 minutes   Serves 6–8

HOT GARLIC CHEESE PUFFS
INGREDIENTS
CHOUX PASTRY
Water	125 ml
Butter	30 g
Salt	⅛ tsp
Plain (all-purpose) flour	80 g, sifted
Eggs	2, about 60 g each, lightly beaten

FILLING
Butter	30 g
Plain (all-purpose) flour	1 Tbsp
Milk	125 ml
Cheddar cheese	2 Tbsp, grated
Parmesan cheese	1 Tbsp
Spring onions (scallions)	2 Tbsp, chopped
Parsley	1 Tbsp, chopped
Garlic	2 Tbsp, peeled, chopped and fried
Tomato	1 Tbsp, skin removed and pulped
Salt and freshly ground black pepper	to taste

METHOD
CHOUX PASTRY
- Combine water, butter and salt in a pan and stir until butter melts. Bring mixture to a rolling boil and add in flour all at once.
- Stir vigorously with a wooden spoon until mixture leaves side of pan and forms a smooth dough.
- Remove from heat and cool slightly. Add in beaten eggs a little at a time, beating well with an electric hand mixer after each addition.
- Put heaped teaspoons of pastry on lightly greased oven trays. Allow room for expansion.
- Bake in a preheated oven at 200°C for 25 minutes or until crisp.
- Meanwhile, prepare filling. Melt butter in pan; add flour, sauté for 1 minute, stirring constantly.
- Add in milk and stir until sauce boils and thickens. Add in cheeses.
- Remove from heat; add in spring onions, parsley, garlic and tomato. Season to taste with salt and pepper.
- Cut puffs into halves and remove any soft centre. Leave to cool.
- When ready to serve, spoon filling into puffs.

Chef's Note:
- *Choux pastry can be baked earlier and reheated just before serving. It is also excellent with sweet fillings.*

Preparation time: 15 minutes   Cooking time: 20 minutes   Serves 10–12

COCONUT CHURCH CANDY
INGREDIENTS
Evaporated milk	175 ml
Castor sugar	675 g
Butter	125 g
Salt	¼ tsp
Grated coconut	600 g
Vanilla essence	2 tsp
Green and red food colouring	

METHOD
- Combine evaporated milk and sugar and heat in a heavy-based pan until sugar dissolves.
- Add in butter and salt. Stir to mix.
- Stir to mix. Add in grated coconut and stir mixture until it starts to leave the sides of pan. Divide mixture into 2 portions and add green colouring to one and red colouring to the other. Stir until colour is well-incorporated.
- Quickly press candy down firmly, with the back of a spoon or a banana leaf if easily available, into greased 15 x 15-cm cake pans.
- Cut out required sizes with a sharp knife while mixture is still hot.
- Allow to cool overnight before serving.

Chef's Note:
- *To make coconut candy, always use a heavy-based pan to prevent candy from burning.*

From top: Coconut Church Candy; Hot Garlic Cheese Puffs

Preparation time: 25 minutes Cooking time: 15 minutes Serves 4–6

FRIED CRISPY WANTONS

INGREDIENTS

Minced chicken	300 g
Prawns (shrimps)	500 g, shelled and finely cubed
Salt	1 tsp
Ground white pepper	1 tsp
Sugar	1 tsp
Sesame oil	½ tsp
Egg	1, separated
Wanton wrappers	185 g
Cooking oil	500 ml for deep-frying

SWEET SOUR SAUCE

White vinegar	4 Tbsp
Sugar	3 Tbsp
Tomato sauce	4 Tbsp
Water	4 Tbsp
Salt	½ tsp
Light soy sauce	2 tsp
Cornflour (cornstarch)	1½ tsp

METHOD

- Combine chicken, prawns, salt, pepper, sugar, sesame oil and egg yolk in a deep bowl. Mix thoroughly until mixture is well combined.
- Place 1 heaped tsp of mixture in the centre of a wanton wrapper. Brush edges with lightly beaten egg white. Fold wrapper in half diagonally to shape into a triangle and pinch edges together gently but firmly. Gather small pleats in wrapper just above filling. Repeat process with remaining wanton wrappers and filling.
- Heat oil and deep-fry a few wantons at a time. Drain on absorbent paper.
- Prepare the sweet sour sauce. Mix the ingredients in a small saucepan and stir over low heat until sauce boils and thickens. There should be enough sauce for about 36–40 wantons. Serve in a separate bowl with the wantons.

Chef's Note:
- *For better texture, rub fresh prawns with a little cornstarch and salt before using.*
- *You may substitute chicken with other meats of your choice.*
- *These wantons can also be served with a hot chilli sauce.*

Preparation time: 15 minutes Cooking time: 10 minutes Serves 6–8

CURRIED EGG AND CUCUMBER SANDWICHES

INGREDIENTS

Wholemeal bread	8 slices
Butter	40 g, softened
Hardboiled eggs	3
Mayonnaise	60 ml
Curry powder	1 tsp
Chopped tomatoes	2 Tbsp
Cucumber slices	a few

METHOD

- Spread each slice of bread with 1 tsp butter. Mash eggs then stir in mayonnaise, curry powder and tomatoes.
- Spread 4 bread slices with egg mixture and top with cucumber slices. Sandwich with remaining bread slices.
- Trim crusts and cut into triangles.

From top: Curried Egg and Cucumber Sandwiches; Fried Crispy Wantons

Preparation time: 20 minutes   Cooking time: 40 minutes   Serves 8–12

CHOCOLATE-DIPPED SHORTBREAD FINGERS

INGREDIENTS

Butter	250 g, softened
Castor sugar	70 g
Plain (all-purpose) flour	330 g, sifted with 30 g rice flour
Vanilla essence	1 tsp

CHOCOLATE DIP

Chocolate	90 g, melted with 30 g of shortening or butter

METHOD

- Cream butter and castor sugar in a small bowl with an electric mixer until light and fluffy.
- Stir in sifted flour and rice flour in two batches.
- Transfer mixture to a lightly floured surface. Knead lightly until smooth.
- Press mixture evenly over the base of a 19 x 29-cm lamington pan and prick well with a fork. Mark into fingers of desired size.
- Bake in a preheated oven at 150°C for about 40 minutes, or until lightly browned. Let shortbread stand for a few minutes then cut into fingers and leave to cool.
- Line a wire rack with greaseproof paper.
- Dip half of each shortbread finger into chocolate dip. Shake off excess chocolate and leave to set on rack at room temperature.

Chef's Note:

- *Rice flour can be substituted with ground rice, if desired.*
- *Shortbread can be stored in an airtight container for 2 weeks or frozen for 2 months.*
- *Instead of dipping into chocolate, you can also drizzle the chocolate onto the shortbread fingers. A combination of both white and dark chocolate is brilliant.*

Preparation time: 30 minutes   Serves 8–10

MINT TOMATOES

INGREDIENTS

Cherry tomatoes	24, firm and of same size
Cream cheese	125 g
Butter	30 g
Finely chopped mint	30 g
Mustard	1 tsp
Salt	½ tsp
Freshly ground white pepper	1 tsp
Grated Parmesan cheese	2 Tbsp

METHOD

- Cut tops off tomatoes. Scoop out some of the flesh with a teaspoon. Set aside.
- Beat cream cheese and butter together until smooth. Add finely chopped mint, mustard, salt, freshly ground white pepper and grated Parmesan cheese.
- Pipe small rosettes of cream cheese mixture into each tomato. Refrigerate until firm.
- Remove from refrigerator 30 minutes before serving.

Chef's Note:

- *If cherry tomatoes are not available, use regular tomatoes but of smaller size, which can be put into the mouth in one bite.*
- *As a variation to this recipe, tuna, salmon or even pepperoni can be added to the filling.*

From left: Chocolate-dipped Shortbread Fingers; Mint Tomatoes

Preparation time: 15 minutes   Cooking time: 15 minutes   Serves 4–6

CUSTARD PRAWN FRITTERS

INGREDIENTS

Custard powder	50 g
Self-raising flour	200 g
Bicarbonate of soda	1 tsp
Egg	1
Chicken stock granules	1½ tsp, mixed with 200 ml water
Prawns (shrimps)	250 g, shelled
Freshly ground black pepper	1 tsp
Onion	1, large, peeled and thinly sliced
Red chillies	4, thinly sliced
Spring onions (scallions)	2 sprigs, cut into 3-cm lengths
Cooking oil for deep-frying	

METHOD
- Mix custard powder, self-raising flour, bicarbonate of soda and egg in a bowl.
- Add in chicken stock mixture and mix into a smooth batter.
- Add in prawns, pepper, onion, chillies and spring onions. Mix well.
- Heat oil in a wok. Drop tablespoonful of mixture into hot oil. Fry until golden brown. Drain well on absorbent paper.
- Serve with Thousand Island dressing.

Chef's Note:
- *As a variation to this recipe, other vegetables such as aubergines (eggplants/brinjals) can be thinly cut and added to the batter before frying.*

Preparation time: 25 minutes   Cooking time: 10 minutes   Serves 6–8

PLATTER OF PEANUT CRACKERS AND DIPS

INGREDIENTS

Peanuts (groundnuts)	200 g, roasted

BATTER

Rice flour	100 g
Cornflour (cornstarch)	2 Tbsp
Curry powder	1 tsp
Salt	1 tsp
Water	200 ml
Shallots	5–6, peeled and sliced
Garlic	2 cloves, peeled and minced
Cooking oil for deep-frying	

METHOD

- Mix all batter ingredients and set aside. Add all the peanuts to batter.
- Heat oil in a wok until smoking hot. Using a medium-sized ladle, spoon the peanut batter into the side of the wok, just below the oil, so that the fritters turn golden in colour.
- Drain onto kitchen towels.

TUNA DIP

Tuna	2 cans, drained
Kaffir lime leaves (*daun limau purut*)	2 pieces, finely chopped
Lemon grass (*serai*)	2 stalks, finely chopped
Cream cheese	2 Tbsp
Mayonnaise	2 Tbsp
Dijon mustard	1 tsp
Lemon juice	1 Tbsp
Freshly ground black pepper	1 tsp
Salt	¼ tsp
Bird's eye chillies	2–4, optional

METHOD

- Mix all the above ingredients together and set aside.

AUBERGINE DIP

Aubergines (eggplants/brinjals)	2–3
Mint leaves	a few sprigs
Red chilli	1, finely minced
Green chilli	1, finely minced
Onion	1, peeled and finely minced
Lime or lemon juice	1–2 Tbsp
Yoghurt or sour cream	2 Tbsp
Salt, sugar and pepper	to taste
Olive oil	1 Tbsp

METHOD

- Heat oven and grill aubergines until skin is charred. Remove and plunge into ice cold water. Peel away the outer skin and discard.
- Mash the flesh using a fork. Add in the rest of the ingredients and mix well. Season to taste with salt, sugar and pepper.

Preparation time: 15 minutes Cooking time: 15 minutes Serves 8–10

MALAYSIAN PEANUT BUTTER & CORN PANCAKES (*APAM BALIK*)

INGREDIENTS

Water	300 ml
Castor sugar	50 g
Plain (all-purpose) flour	200 g, sifted together with 50 g cornflour (cornstarch)
Egg	1
Bicarbonate of soda	1½ tsp
Salt	½ tsp
Dry yeast	1½ tsp
Butter	125 g

FILLING
Peanut butter
Cream corn

METHOD
- Mix water and sugar. Stir well until sugar dissolves.
- Combine plain flour with cornflour and break egg in the centre of the flour. Add in sugar water and stir until well mixed. Add in bicarbonate of soda, salt and yeast. Mix well.
- Allow to rest for 30 minutes or until frothy.
- Heat a non-stick pan and brush with a little butter.
- Using a ladle 6-cm in diameter, scoop mixture into the heated pan. Spread evenly using the back of the ladle. Cover the pan and cook for a few minutes. Remove.
- Spread peanut butter and cream corn on pancake then fold and serve.

Chef's Note:
- *For an extra touch, add a dollop of any flavoured ice cream to this pancake.*
- *For a savoury pancake, prepare the pancake as above but fill with grated carrots, lettuce and roasted meat.*

Preparation time: 25 minutes Cooking time: 15 minutes Serves 8–10

FRIED MOZZARELLA IN COUSCOUS

INGREDIENTS

Mozzarella cheese	250 g
Plain (all-purpose) flour	125 g
Eggs	3, small
Garlic	1 clove, peeled and grated
Couscous	150 g
Breadcrumbs	50 g
Parmesan cheese	20 g, grated
Shredded fresh basil	7 g
Cooking oil for deep-frying	

SPICY TOMATO SAUCE

Red chillies	3, finely sliced
Tomatoes	1 can (425 g)
Garlic	2 cloves, peeled and crushed
Tomato sauce	60 g
Chilli sauce	60 g
Freshly ground black pepper	1 tsp

METHOD
- Cut Mozzarella into 1.5 x 1.5-cm cubes. Toss cubes in flour then shake away excess flour.
- Dip into combined eggs and garlic. Coat in combined couscous, breadcrumbs, Parmesan cheese and basil; press on firmly. Repeat coating process.
- Place on a tray and refrigerate for 30 minutes.
- Meanwhile, prepare spicy tomato sauce. Place all ingredients in a blender and blend until smooth.
- Pour into a pan and simmer for 8–10 minutes or until slightly thickened.
- Just before serving, deep-fry coated Mozzarella cubes in hot oil in batches until golden brown. Drain on absorbent paper.
- Serve with spicy tomato sauce.

Chef's Note:
- *Prepare Mozzarella balls and refrigerate overnight. It is easier to handle and the coating will set in.*
- *When deep-frying, make sure that oil is not very hot to prevent overcooking.*

From left: Malaysian Peanut Butter & Corn Pancakes (Apam Balik); Fried Mozzarella in Couscous

Preparation time: 20 minutes   Serves 6–8

CHIPOLATA WITH CHEESE AND HAM WRAPS

INGREDIENTS

Chicken or beef cocktail sausages	12 slices
Cheese slices	2–3 slices
Ham (pork, chicken or turkey)	2–3 slices
Skewers	

METHOD

- Deep-fry or boil the cocktail sausages. Drain and set aside.
- Cut the cheese slices into thin strips. Cut the ham slices into slightly thinner strips than the cheese slices.
- Roll a slice of cheese with a slice of ham around a cocktail sausage and skewer it to secure. Repeat with the remaining ingredients. Serve as desired with chilli sauce or a mustard dip.

Preparation time: 15 minutes   Serves 8–10

AVOCADO ANCHOVY DIP ON CRACKERS

INGREDIENTS

Avocado	1, sliced, pitted, peeled and mashed
Anchovy fillets or Oscar sardines	1 can (155 g), drained
Garlic	1, peeled and finely chopped
Red capsicum (bell pepper)	1, finely chopped
Shallots	2–3, peeled and finely chopped
Sour cream	2–3 Tbsp
Lemon juice	1 Tbsp
Coarsely pounded black pepper	1 tsp

GARNISH

Parsley	
Quail eggs	8–12, hardboiled and cut into halves
Crackers	

METHOD

- Combine all the ingredients in a bowl. Season to taste. Cover and refrigerate for 3 hours. Serve with crackers or as desired. Garnish with egg halves and top with parsley.

From top: Avocado Anchovy Dip on Crackers; Chipolata with Cheese and Ham Wraps

Preparation time: 20 minutes   Cooking time: 15 minutes   Serves 4–6

BBQ HOT AND SPICY PRAWNS

INGREDIENTS

Tiger prawns	800 g, cleaned with shell intact

MARINADE

Shallots	6, peeled and minced
Garlic	2 cloves, peeled and minced
Red chilli	2, blended
Freshly ground black pepper	1 tsp
Lemon juice	2 Tbsp
Tomato sauce	2 Tbsp
Oyster sauce	2 Tbsp
Mayonnaise	1 Tbsp
Mint leaves	15 g

METHOD

- Mix together all marinade ingredients and place prawns in. Leave for 1 hour.
- Grill, barbecue or shallow-fry prawns until done.
- Simmer remainder of the marinade and serve with prawns.

Preparation time: 20 minutes   Serves 4–6

PINWHEEL CHEESE AND WALNUT SANDWICHES

INGREDIENTS

White or brown bread	1 loaf (420 g)

FILLING

Cream cheese	250 g
Fresh dates	100 g, sliced, pitted and finely chopped
Walnuts	100 g, finely chopped
Grated orange rind	1 tsp
Orange juice	2 Tbsp

METHOD

- Trim crust from bread then cut bread slices into long slices.
- Combine cream cheese, dates, walnuts, orange rind and orange juice.
- Spread filling evenly onto each long slice; roll up from either long or short side of bread.
- Wrap in cling film and refrigerate for 1 hour.
- Slice into rounds using a serrated knife.

From top: BBQ Hot and Spicy Prawns; Pinwheel Cheese and Walnut Sandwiches

Preparation time: 30 minutes   Cooking time: 10–15 minutes   Serves 6–8

VIENNESE ALMOND CRESCENTS

INGREDIENTS

Almonds	100 g, ground
Plain (all-purpose) flour	280 g, sifted
Castor sugar	70 g
Salt	a pinch
Butter	200 g
Eggs yolks	2

COATING

Vanilla sugar	75 g
Icing (confectioners') sugar	25 g, sifted

METHOD
- Place all dry ingredients except coating ingredients in a mixing bowl. Add in butter and egg yolks. Knead into a soft dough.
- Wrap in foil or cling film and refrigerate for 2 hours.
- Preheat the oven to 180°C.
- Divide dough into small pieces and roll each piece to the thickness of a pencil.
- Cut up rolls into 5-cm pieces and curve each piece into a crescent.
- Place on lightly greased baking trays. Bake in the centre of the oven for 10 minutes or until golden.
- Mix vanilla sugar with icing sugar and toss biscuits in mixture while still warm. Place on racks to cool.

Chef's Note:
- *Hazelnuts can be used instead of almonds.*

Preparation time: 30 minutes Cooking time: 8–10 minutes Serves 6–8

MEXICAN NACHOS

INGREDIENTS

Red kidney beans	1 can (270 g), coarsely puréed
Onion	1, small, peeled and chopped
Garlic	2 cloves, peeled and chopped
Cumin powder	1 tsp
Butter	2 Tbsp, melted
Tomatoes	2, chopped + extra for topping
Red chillies	4, seeded and chopped
Salt and freshly ground black pepper	to taste
Plain corn chips	1 packet (250 g)
Grated Cheddar cheese	60 g
Shredded fresh coriander leaves	1 Tbsp

MEXICAN SALSA

Olive oil	6 Tbsp
Tomatoes	8, large, peeled and chopped
Onions	2, medium, peeled and grated
Garlic	2 cloves, peeled and grated
Fresh green chillies	4, seeded and chopped
Chopped fresh coriander	20 g
Tomato sauce	50 g
Salt and sugar	to taste

METHOD

- Combine beans, onion, garlic, cumin powder, melted butter, tomatoes, red chillies and season with salt and pepper.
- Select unbroken chips and place on a lightly greased baking tray.
- Top corn chips with combined bean mixture then sprinkle with grated cheese.
- Just before serving, bake in a preheated oven at 180°C for about 8–10 minutes or until cheese is melted and chips crisp.
- Top with extra tomato and coriander.

MEXICAN SALSA

METHOD

- Heat oil in a heavy base pan. Add tomatoes, onions, garlic and green chillies. Bring slowly to the boil and cook, stirring frequently over moderate heat until thick and well blended.
- Stir in coriander and cook for 1 more minute.
- Cool slightly, pour into small jars and seal. It is best kept in the refrigerator.

Chef's Note:

- It is easier to peel off tomato skins after the tomatoes have been placed in boiling water for a few minutes.

Preparation time: 15 minutes   Cooking time: 25 minutes   Serves 6–8

BRANDY SNAPS

INGREDIENTS

Butter	50 g
Brown sugar	65 g
Golden syrup	80 ml
Ground ginger	½ tsp
Plain (all-purpose) flour	75 g, sifted
White chocolate	100 g

CREAM FILLING

| Whipped cream | 300 ml, mixed together with 4 Tbsp |
| Bailey's Irish cream | |

METHOD

- Combine butter, sugar, golden syrup and ginger in a pan, stir over low heat without boiling, until butter is melted. Remove from heat, stir in flour.
- Drop teaspoonsful of mixture on lightly greased baking trays.
- For easy handling, bake only three snaps at a time. Bake in a preheated oven at 180°C for 5–6 minutes or until snaps are bubbling and lightly browned.
- Using a metal spatula, quickly lift brandy snaps from tray. Roll each snap immediately around handle of a wooden spoon. Slip snap from spoon handle and place on a wire rack to cool.
- Prepare cream filling. Beat together whipped cream and Bailey's Irish cream until firm.
- Just before serving, spoon filling into piping bag fitted with a small star nozzle. Pipe filling into snaps.

Chef's Note:

- Bake about 3 snaps at a time until you become adept at rolling them. This recipe needs practice and patience.
- Unfilled brandy snaps keep well in airtight containers.
- After rolling onto wooden spoons, chill in the freezer for 2–3 seconds. Place in paper cups and chill in the refrigerator until required.

Preparation time: 30 minutes   Cooking time: 30 minutes   Serves 6–10

MINI HERB AND GARLIC SANDWICHES

INGREDIENTS

HERB AND GARLIC BREAD

Plain (all-purpose) flour	600 g
Butter	50 g
Castor sugar	50 g
Salt	1 tsp
Mixed herbs	2 Tbsp
Garlic	2 cloves, peeled and finely chopped
Dry yeast	11 g
Egg	1, lightly beaten + 1 for egg wash
Fresh milk	300 g, lukewarm

METHOD

- Sieve plain flour into a bowl, add butter and rub in flour. Add in sugar, salt, herbs, garlic and yeast. Add in beaten egg and warm milk.
- Mix with a wooden spoon. Knead until a soft dough is formed.
- Allow to rest until it doubles in size. Punch down, knead and remould.
- Divide into 6 portions. Roll and shape into 20-cm long cylinders. Plait 3 of them into a loaf, making 2 loaves altogether.
- Place on lightly greased baking trays and allow to prove for 15–20 minutes.
- Bake at 220°C for 20–25 minutes.
- Brush bread with egg wash halfway through baking.
- When done, cut into thin slices and serve with the following toppings and seasonings.

TOPPINGS

Roast beef	120 g
Prawns (shrimps)	50 g, boiled and blanched in cold water
Pineapple	115 g
Banana	50 g, rubbed with lemon juice

SEASONINGS
Mustard
Mango chutney
Peanut butter

Chef's Note:

- *To obtain very soft dough, dough can be kept in the refrigerator overnight, then punched down and remoulded.*

Preparation time: 15 minutes   Cooking time: 15 minutes   Serves 6–12

GRILLED ORANGE CHICKEN BITES
INGREDIENTS

MARINADE
Orange juice	1 Tbsp
Honey	1 tsp
Garlic	1 clove, peeled and grated
Ginger	0.5-cm knob, peeled and grated
Shallots	2, peeled and grated
Salt and freshly ground black pepper	to taste
Butter or olive oil	2 Tbsp
Chicken	350 g, deboned and sliced

GARNISH
Orange slices	sliced to 1-cm thickness
Red chilli	
Spring onions (scallions)	

METHOD
- Combine marinade ingredients and place chicken slices in for a few hours.
- Heat grill to 180°C. Place chicken pieces into a baking tray and brush with butter. Grill until cooked.
- Place the grilled chicken pieces onto the orange slices. Garnish with red chilli and spring onions. Serve with cocktail drinks.

Preparation time: 15 minutes   Cooking time: 20 minutes   Serves 6–8

CHEESE ALMOND FINGERS
INGREDIENTS

Butter	250 g
Granulated sugar	50 g
Salt	1 tsp
Egg	1, lightly beaten + 1 for glazing
Parmesan cheese	200 g, grated
Ground almonds	100 g
Plain (all-purpose) flour	300 g
Almond nibs	

METHOD
- Beat butter, sugar, salt and egg until creamy.
- Add in grated cheese, ground almonds and then mix in flour and blend well into a soft dough.
- Roll out dough to 7-mm in thickness and cut into strips measuring 0.5 x 6-cm. Place on a greased baking tray.
- Brush with egg glaze.
- Sprinkle almond nibs.
- Bake in a preheated oven at 180°C for 20 minutes until golden brown.

Chef's Note:
- As an alternative, walnuts or any other desired groundnuts can be used in place of almonds. Sesame seeds can be used instead of almond nibs.

Centre: Cheese Almond Fingers; Around: Grilled Orange Chicken Bites

Preparation time: 30 minutes   Cooking time: 25 minutes   Serves 4–12

APPLE WALNUT MUFFINS

INGREDIENTS

Butter	for greasing

INGREDIENTS A

Plain (all-purpose) flour	180 g
Baking powder	1 tsp
Cinnamon powder	½ tsp
Salt	¼ tsp

INGREDIENTS B

Castor sugar	200 g
Vegetable oil	125 ml
Egg	1, large
Lemon rind	from 1 lemon
Lemon juice	2 Tbsp
Vanilla essence	1 tsp
Green apples	2, skinned and grated
Semolina	2 Tbsp
Walnuts	50 g, toasted

METHOD

- Grease a muffin pan with butter. Set aside.
- Sift together Ingredients A; set aside.
- In a bowl, combine Ingredients B until well mixed. Fold in Ingredients A.
- Stir in apples, semolina and toasted walnuts.
- Spoon mixture into greased muffin pan until each cup is two-thirds full then spread evenly. Bake in a preheated oven at 180°C for 25 minutes or until done. Remove from pan and cool on a wire rack.

Preparation time: 20 minutes   Cooking time: 15 minutes   Serves 4–6

CURRY PUFFS

INGREDIENTS

SHORT CRUST PASTRY

Plain (all-purpose) flour	250 g
Salt	½ tsp
Vegetable shortening	40 g
Margarine	50 g
Cold water	4–6 Tbsp

FILLING

Cooking oil	
Onion	1, large, peeled and finely chopped
Ginger	1-cm knob, peeled and finely chopped
Garlic	2 cloves, peeled and finely chopped
Curry leaves	1 sprig, finely chopped
Potato	1, peeled and cubed
Chicken	250 g, deboned and cubed
Meat curry powder	2 Tbsp
Salt and freshly ground black pepper	to taste

METHOD

- Make short crust pastry by rubbing-in method. Sieve flour and salt in a mixing bowl. Rub in vegetable shortening and margarine using fingertips until the mixture resembles fine breadcrumbs.
- Add in cold water but care should be taken not to add too much water. Gently mix in the cold water and draw pastry together. Knead lightly and turn onto a lightly floured board. Rest pastry in refrigerator for 30 minutes.
- Meanwhile prepare filling. Heat a non-stick pan with oil, and sauté chopped ingredients.
- Add in potato cubes and stir-fry to cook. Sprinkle a little water every now and then.
- Add in chicken and curry powder. Season to taste and allow excess liquid to dry up. Allow filling to cool.
- Roll out pastry to 2-mm thickness and cut out rounds with a 10-cm round pastry cutter.
- Place 1 Tbsp filling on each round and dampen edges with water.
- Fold pastry over to enclose filling and pinch the edges to seal. Repeat process until all the filling is used up.
- Heat oil and deep-fry a few curry puffs at a time. Drain and serve hot with chilli sauce if desired.

Chef's Note:

- *For filling, any other meat or seafood can be used.*
- *Pastry can be prepared beforehand. Curry puffs can be made a day in advance and frozen. Deep-fry just before serving.*

From top: Curry Puffs; Apple Walnut Muffins

43

Preparation time: 20 minutes   Cooking time: 10–15 minutes   Serves 4–6

SPICED LAMB KOFTA

INGREDIENTS

Minced lamb	600 g
Onion	1, peeled and grated
Garlic	1 clove, peeled and grated
Grated lime rind	1 tsp
Ground cumin	1 tsp
Ground coriander	1 tsp
Chilli powder	1 tsp
Shredded mint leaves	1 Tbsp
Salt	1 tsp
Bamboo skewers, sugarcane sticks or lemon grass stalks	

YOGHURT DIP

Yoghurt	250 g
Shredded mint leaves	2 Tbsp
Chilli sauce	1 Tbsp
Salt	½ tsp
Lemon juice	1 Tbsp

METHOD
- Combine all ingredients in a bowl; mix well. Cover and refrigerate for 1 hour.
- Shape 1 Tbsp of mixture around end of each skewer.
- Place under the grill or cook on oiled griddle pan.
- Prepare yoghurt dip. Combine all ingredients in a jar and serve with hot Koftas.

Chef's Note:
- *Soak bamboo skewers in water for 1 hour before using to prevent burning. Instead of skewers, sugarcane sticks or lemon grass stalks can also be used.*
- *Koftas can be prepared a day in advance.*
- *Fresh fruits can be skewered on as garnish.*

Preparation time: 20 minutes   Cooking time: 10 minutes   Serves 8–10

COCONUT SQUARES

INGREDIENTS

Butter	60 g
Plain cooking chocolate	80 g
Desiccated coconut	150 g
Condensed milk	170 g
Vanilla essence	1 tsp
Golden raisins	200 g
Red glacé cherries	10, thickly sliced
Green glacé cherries	10, thickly sliced

METHOD
- Line a 14 x 10-cm baking tray with aluminium foil. Set aside.
- Melt butter and cooking chocolate in a basin over hot water.
- Add in rest of the ingredients and mix well to combine.
- Press mixture into prepared trays firmly and refrigerate overnight.
- Cut into dainty small squares.

Chef's Note:
- *For a mocha flavour, dissolve 2 tsp of coffee powder and 1 tsp of coffee liqueur and add to the mixture.*
- *White chocolate can be used instead of plain cooking chocolate.*

Preparation time: 10 minutes   Cooking time: 15 minutes   Serves 6–8

MINI POPIAHS

INGREDIENTS

Small spring roll wraps	1 packet (125 g)
Plain (all-purpose) flour	1 Tbsp, mixed with 2 tsp water

FILLING

Cooking oil	
Shallots	4, peeled and chopped
Garlic	4 cloves, peeled and chopped
Prawns (shrimps)	150 g, shelled, cleaned and chopped
Crabmeat	150 g, shredded
Dried Chinese mushrooms	3, soaked and finely sliced
Turnip	1, small, skinned and shredded
Carrot	1, skinned and shredded
Soft bean curd (*tofu*)	1, cubed
Salt and freshly ground black pepper	to taste

METHOD

- Prepare the filling. Heat 2–3 Tbsp oil in a pan and stir-fry shallots and garlic. Add in prawns, crabmeat and mushrooms. Stir-fry until dry. Add in turnip, carrot and bean curd. Stir-fry for a few seconds. Season to taste. Dish out and allow to cool. Drain off excess liquid.
- Place 1 Tbsp of filling across two opposite corners of a wrapper. Brush edges with a little flour paste and tuck in ends. Roll up to enclose filling. Repeat until all the filling is used up.
- Deep-fry spring rolls in batches in hot oil until lightly browned and cooked through. Drain on absorbent paper. Serve with a chilli sauce.

Preparation time: 25 minutes   Cooking time: 20 minutes   Serves 6–8

CHERRY NUT BISCUITS

INGREDIENTS

Butter	125 g
Vanilla essence	1 tsp
Castor sugar	50 g
Egg	1, lightly beaten
Self-raising flour	150 g, sifted
Almond nibs	125 g
Glacé cherries	16, halved

METHOD

- Cream butter, vanilla essence and castor sugar until light and fluffy. Add egg a little at a time. Beat well to mix.
- Add flour and mix to a soft dough.
- Drop 1 rounded tsp of mixture into almond nibs. Roll into balls. Flatten and press a cherry half on top of each.
- Put on a lightly greased baking tray; allow room for spreading. Bake in a preheated oven at 170–180°C for 15–20 minutes or until golden. Cool on a wire rack.

From top: Mini Popiahs; Cherry Nut Biscuits

Preparation time: 30 minutes   Cooking time: 15 minutes   Serves 4–6

BARBECUED CHICKEN SKEWERS

INGREDIENTS

Chicken	600 g, deboned and cut into 3-cm pieces
Lemon grass (*serai*)	4 stalks, coarsely pounded
Fresh turmeric root	2.5-cm knob, coarsely pounded
Garlic	2 cloves, peeled and coarsely pounded
Salt	2 tsp
Sugar	1 Tbsp
Tamarind juice	1 Tbsp
Bamboo skewers	30, soaked in water for a few hours

PEANUT SAUCE

Dried chillies	15, soaked
Garlic	3 cloves, peeled
Shallots	12, peeled
Lemon grass (*serai*)	3 stalks, cut into 4-cm lengths
Candlenuts	5
Chicken stock granules	1 Tbsp
Ground coriander	1 Tbsp, finely blended
Ground cumin	1 tsp
Ground fennel	1 tsp
Tamarind pulp	2 Tbsp
Salt	1½ tsp
Sugar	5 tsp
Peanuts (groundnuts)	180 g, coarsely pounded
Coconut milk	60 ml

METHOD

- Marinate chicken pieces with all the pounded ingredients and season to taste with salt, sugar and tamarind juice.
- Skewer meat onto bamboo skewers and set aside.
- Prepare peanut sauce. Blend dried chillies, garlic, shallots, lemon grass, candlenuts and chicken stock granules until fine.
- Heat a pot with a little oil and stir blended ingredients, ground coriander, ground cumin and ground fennel until aromatic.
- Add in sufficient water, tamarind pulp and season to taste with salt and sugar. Simmer and lastly add in peanuts and coconut milk.
- Heat a grill and grill the skewers. Alternatively, barbecue skewers on a bed of hot coals. Baste and turn once or twice with oil and coconut milk. Serve hot.

Chef's Note:
- As a variation to this recipe, beef, pork or mutton can be used instead of chicken.

Preparation time: 15 minutes   Cooking time: 15 minutes   Serves 6–8

TROPICAL COCONUT PRAWNS WITH MANGO SAUCE

INGREDIENTS

Prawns (shrimps)	500 g, large, shelled except for tails and deveined
Salt and freshly ground black pepper	to taste
Cornflour (cornstarch)	
Egg white	1, lightly beaten
Shredded coconut	70 g
Cooking oil for deep-frying	

MANGO SAUCE

Mango slices	400 g
Thousand Island dressing	3 Tbsp
Mango chutney	3 Tbsp
Freshly ground black pepper	1 tsp

METHOD

- Rub prawns with a little salt and pepper then toss in cornflour and shake away excess. Dip prawns in the egg white, then coconut.
- Just before serving, deep-fry the prawns in hot oil until light brown in colour. Serve with mango sauce.
- To make mango sauce, blend all the ingredients together until smooth.

Chef's Note:
- Prawns and sauce can be prepared and refrigerated a day earlier.
- If shredded coconut is not easily available, shred a fresh coconut kernel at home.
- To add spice to the flavour, rub 1 tsp of chilli powder onto the prawns.

Preparation time: 20 minutes   Cooking time: 20 minutes   Serves 6–8

BLUEBERRY CHEESE TARTLETS
INGREDIENTS
PASTRY
Butter	125 g
Castor sugar	80 g
Egg	1
Plain (all-purpose) flour	250 g, sifted
Salt	a pinch

CREAM CHEESE FILLING
Cream cheese	250 g
Sour cream	125 ml
Sugar	60 g
Lemon juice	2 Tbsp
Lemon rind	1 tsp
Egg	1, small

TOPPING
Blueberries	
Strawberries	
Kiwi fruit	skinned and cut into slices
Mandarin	peeled and broken into segments

METHOD
PASTRY
- Cream butter and sugar until light and fluffy. Add in egg and beat to mix well. Add in flour to make a soft dough.
- Roll out dough. Line patty tins with pastry and prick holes with a fork.

- Prepare cream cheese filling. Mix all the ingredients together into a smooth batter.
- Blind bake the pastry for 15 minutes in a preheated oven at 180°C then leave to cool. Fill with cream cheese filling.
- Bake in a preheated oven at 180°C for 10–15 minutes. Top with different fruits.

Preparation time: 15 minutes   Cooking time: 20 minutes   Serves 4–6

LAMB MEATBALLS WITH CREAMY MINT SAUCE
INGREDIENTS
Minced (ground) lamb	500 g
Onion	1, large, peeled and chopped
Ginger	2 tsp, peeled and grated
Ground cumin	2 tsp
Curry powder	1 tsp
Tomato paste	1 Tbsp
Breadcrumbs	70 g
Salt and freshly ground black pepper	to taste
Cooking oil for shallow-frying	

CREAMY MINT SAUCE
Sour cream	125 ml
Mayonnaise	125 ml
Chopped mint leaves	2 Tbsp

METHOD
- Blend all the ingredients except oil until they form a smooth paste.
- Shape 1 Tbsp of mixture into a ball using damp hands. Repeat until all the mixture is used up.
* Shallow-fry meatballs in batches in hot oil until cooked through.

CREAMY MINT SAUCE
- Combine all the ingredients in a bowl.
- Serve with creamy mint sauce.

Chef's Note:
- *Receipe can be prepared a day ahead. Meatballs are suitable for freezing.*

From top: Blueberry Cheese Tartlets; Lamb Meatballs with Creamy Mint Sauce

51

Preparation time: 20 minutes   Cooking time: 15 minutes   Serves 10–12

PALMIERS WITH CUCUMBER DIP

INGREDIENTS

Ready rolled puff pastry	375 g
SWEET POTATO FILLING	
Sweet potato (Kumara)	320 g, boiled and mashed
Garlic	1 clove, peeled and minced
Melted butter	2 tsp
Sun-dried tomatoes in oil	½ cup, drained and chopped
Fresh basil	2 Tbsp
Salt and freshly ground black pepper	to taste

METHOD
- Combine all the sweet potato filling ingredients in a bowl and set aside.
- Spread half of the filling on 1 sheet of pastry.
- Fold in sides to meet at the centre, flatten slightly; press sides together. Cover and refrigerate for an hour.
- Cut pastry into 1.5-cm slices; place, cut-side up, on lightly greased baking trays.
- Bake in a preheated oven at 170–180°C for about 15 minutes.
- Serve with a dip or chilli sauce.

Chef's Note:
- *Palmiers can be prepared in advance. Place on prepared oven trays, cover with aluminium foil and refrigerate. Bake as close to serving time as possible.*

Preparation time: 15 minutes   Cooking time: 20 minutes   Serves 4–6

Cucumber Dip

INGREDIENTS

Cucumber	1, small, skinned and diced
Granny Smith apple	1, skinned, cored and diced
Mayonnaise	3 Tbsp
Yoghurt	3 Tbsp
Chilli sauce	1 Tbsp
Lemon juice	1 tsp
Salt and pepper	to taste

METHOD
- Mix all the ingredients in a blender or food processor and process until smooth.

Preparation time: 30 minutes   Cooking time: 10 minutes   Serves 8–10

MINI COLD CUTS AND SEAFOOD TERRINES

INGREDIENTS

Agar-agar powder	10 g, softened
Clear chicken stock	1 litre
Salt	1 tsp
Lemon juice	2 Tbsp
Prawns (shrimps)	6–8 pieces, boiled and blanched
Green peas	4 Tbsp, boiled and blanched
Corn kernels	4 Tbsp, boiled and blanched
Asparagus sticks	4–6 pieces, boiled and blanched
Kiwi fruit cubes	3 Tbsp
Pineapple cubes	3 Tbsp
Mango	3 Tbsp
COLD CUTS	
Chicken ham	a few slices
Pepperoni	a few slices
Smoked salmon	a few slices

METHOD
- Dissolve agar-agar powder in chicken stock and salt. Bring to gentle boil. Season to taste with lemon juice.
- Allow mixture to cool slightly. Pour into moulds then fill moulds with the desired ingredients. Do the same with prawns, vegetables, fruits and cold cuts.
- Chill in the refrigerator. Unmould onto plate and serve.

Chef's Note:
- *A shimmering mould of jellied cold terrines will tempt the most languid summer appetite.*
- *Olives, boiled quails' eggs, nuts, cheese, pickled ginger, mushrooms can be added. Use your favourite ingredients!*
- *There is no doubt that home-made stock is by far the best, but don't go worry if you have to use a stock cube. We all do use it occasionally.*

From top: Palmiers with Cucumber Dip; Mini Cold Cuts and Seafood Terrines

Preparation time: 20 minutes Cooking time: 20 minutes Serves 6–8

SAVOURY MASALA NUTS
INGREDIENTS
Cooking oil	1 Tbsp
Garam masala	1 tsp
Garlic powder	2 tsp
Chilli powder	2 tsp
Roasted almonds	100 g
Roasted cashew nuts	100 g
Roasted pecan nuts	100 g

METHOD
- Place oil, garam masala, garlic powder, chilli powder and nuts into a baking tray. Stir to coat nuts.
- Preheat oven at 160–180°C for 20 minutes before putting in tray. Cook, tossing occasionally for 5 minutes.
- Remove from heat. Cool before serving.

Chef's Note:
- *Garam Masala, a combination of 6 spices, is available from most Indian and Asian food stores.*

Preparation time: 30 minutes Cooking time: 20 minutes Serves 6–8

ALMOND PRAWN TOAST
INGREDIENTS
Prawns (shrimps)	500 g, finely chopped
Garlic	2 cloves, peeled and chopped
Shallots	2 bulbs, peeled and chopped
Ginger	1 tsp, peeled and grated
Sugar	1 tsp
Cornflour (cornstarch)	1 Tbsp
Freshly cracked white pepper	1 tsp
Fish sauce	1 Tbsp
Egg white	1, lightly beaten
Salt	1 tsp
Roughly chopped spring onions (scallions)	2 Tbsp
Red chillies	2, seeded and diced
French loaf	1
Eggs	2, lightly beaten
Almonds	80 g, combined with 80 g breadcrumbs
Cooking oil	500 ml for deep-frying

METHOD
- In a bowl, combine prawns, garlic, shallots, ginger, sugar, cornflour, pepper, fish sauce, egg white and salt until well mixed.
- Mix in spring onions and chillies.
- Cut french loaf diagonally into 1-cm thick slices. Spread 1 Tbsp of prawn mixture on each slice. Brush lightly with beaten egg.
- Coat prawn mixture with combined almonds and breadcrumbs; press firmly onto surface.
- Deep-fry prawn toasts, with prawn-coated side down, in batches until golden brown. Drain on sheets of absorbent paper. Serve as desired with chilli sauce.

Chef's Note:
- *Prawn toast can be prepared and wrapped in foil and frozen. When needed, they can be deep-fried from frozen.*
- *Ordinary bread slices can also be used instead. Cut bread into neat finger slices.*
- *As a variation to this recipe, sesame seeds can be used in place of almonds.*

From top: Savoury Masala Nuts; Almond Prawn Toast

Preparation time: 15 minutes   Cooking time: 15 minutes   Serves 6–8

VEGETABLE TEMPURA WITH MUSTARD DIP
INGREDIENTS
Plain (all-purpose) flour	350 g
Salt	1/2 tsp
Eggs	2, small
Cold water	330 ml
Cooking oil for deep-frying	
Lady's fingers (okra)	9, small
Aubergines (eggplants/brinjals)	2, small, long and cut into sticks
Carrots	2, cut into sticks

MUSTARD DIP
Mayonnaise	250 g
Grainy mustard	2 Tbsp
Wasabi	1/2 tsp
Chopped spring onions (scallions)	2 Tbsp

METHOD
- Heat oil in a wok or pan.
- Meanwhile, sift the flour and salt into a bowl. Set aside.
- Beat eggs until frothy, add in iced water and continue beating for 2–3 minutes. Add in sifted flour and mix lightly.
- Dip vegetables in batter and fry in very hot oil until golden brown. Drain on paper towels.
- Prepare mustard dip. Mix together all the ingredients in a small saucepan and allow the sauce to boil.
- Remove from heat and allow to cool.
- Serve vegetable tempura with mustard dip.

Chef's Note:
- For variety, you may choose to serve this dish with mayonnaise mixed with 3–4 tablespoons of whole grain mustard instead.

Preparation Time: 20 minutes   Cooking Time: 15 minutes   Serves 8–10

FILLED TOP HATS/PIE TEE SHELLS
INGREDIENTS
Rice flour	100 g, sifted together with 30 g plain (all-purpose) flour and 1/2 tsp salt
Egg	1
Coconut milk	180–200 ml

FILLING
Cooking oil	2 Tbsp
Garlic	3 cloves, peeled and finely chopped
Prawns (shrimps)	150 g, shelled and diced
Carrot	1, small, skinned and shredded
Turnip	1, small, skinned and shredded
Sugar	1 tsp
Salt	1 tsp
Freshly ground black pepper	1 tsp
Spring onion (scallion)	1, chopped

METHOD
- To make batter, sift flours and salt into a bowl. Make a well in the centre and pour in egg. Gradually add in coconut milk and mix into a smooth thin batter. Strain and pour into a jug.
- Heat oil in a small deep saucepan over medium heat. Place the pie tee mould into oil. When mould is heated through, lift it out and dip it into the batter until the mould is almost covered entirely. Lift the mould out of the batter and carefully lower the mould into the hot oil.
- Immediately jiggle the mould gently. Shake it off the mould with a skewer and continue frying until crisp and golden brown. Drain on absorbent paper. Repeat until all the batter is used up.
- Cool and store in an airtight container.
- Prepare filling. Heat oil and sauté garlic until golden brown.
- Drain garlic into a saucer. Then fry prawns in the same oil until fragrant. Toss in shredded carrot and turnip. Season to taste with sugar, salt and pepper.
- Add in spring onions and dish out onto a plate. To serve, fill top hats with filling.

Chef's Note:
- For pie tee shells or top hats, you need a special brass mould which can be bought at any Asian supermarket or Chinese sundry shops.
- Always prepare the shells a few days ahead and store in an airtight container.
- Try a variety of fillings. This is a brilliant antipasto to serve for any occasion.

From left: Vegetable Tempura with Mustard Dip; Filled Top Hats/Pie Tee Shells

Preparation time: 30 minutes   Cooking time: 10 minutes   Serves 4–6

SARDINE CONES

INGREDIENTS

| White bread | 8–10 slices |

SARDINE DILL CREAM

Cream cheese	100 g
French Mustard	1 tsp
Chives	1 Tbsp
Parsley	1 Tbsp
Dill	1 Tbsp
Lemon juice	1–2 tsp
Tabasco sauce	a dash or two
Sardines	1 can (155 g)

METHOD

- Heat oven to 170°C. You may also use an oven toaster. Flatten bread slices and roll into cones. Secure with a toothpick and toast bread lightly. Set aside.
- To make sardine dill cream, beat the cream cheese in a small bowl until smooth, add in French mustard, herbs, lemon juice, Tabasco sauce and sardines. Beat until smooth. Season to taste. Cover and refrigerate for 2 hours.
- Just before serving, spoon sardine dill cream into a piping bag fitted with a fluted nozzle, and pipe the filling into the bread cones. Garnish as desired.

Chef's Note:

- As a variation to this recipe, you may add pepper or any other spice that you like to the sardine dill cream to make it spicy.
- Add a touch of caviar to this recipe for something special.

Preparation time: 15 minutes   Cooking time: 10 minutes   Serves 4–6

THAI FISH CAKES WITH CHILLI DIP

INGREDIENTS

Cooking oil for frying	
Green chilli	1, chopped
Red chilli	1, chopped
Lemon grass (*serai*)	1, chopped
Kaffir lime leaf (daun limau purut)	1, chopped
Lemon sole fillet	500 g, finely chopped
Salt	1½ tsp
Freshly ground black pepper	1 tsp
Cornflour (cornstarch)	2 Tbsp
Spring onions (scallions)	2 Tbsp, chopped
Chopped coriander leaves	2 Tbsp
Egg	2, lightly beaten
Breadcrumbs	125 g

CHILLI DIP

Olive oil	1 Tbsp
Curry powder	1 Tbsp
Onion	1, small, peeled and chopped
Mayonnaise	200 g
Chopped mint leaves	30 g
Tomato	1, seeded and chopped
Lime juice	1 Tbsp

METHOD

- Heat oil and fry chillies, lemon grass and kaffir lime leaf for 1 minute. Set aside.
- Place fish in a mixing bowl, mix in salt and pepper, cornflour, spring onions, coriander leaves and fried chilli mixture. Mix.
- Divide mixture into balls and shape into cakes. Cover and chill for 20 minutes.
- Coat cakes in beaten egg, then coat in breadcrumbs. Shallow-fry for 3–4 minutes on each side. Drain well.
- Prepare chilli dip. Heat oil in a non-stick pan and fry the curry powder for a few seconds.
- Add in chopped onions. Allow to cool. Add in the rest of the ingredients and mix together.
- Serve fish cakes with chilli dip.

Preparation time: 30 minutes Cooking time: 20 minutes Serves 8–12

BRUSCHETTA WITH TOPPINGS

INGREDIENTS

French loaves	2, cut into 1-cm slices
Olive oil	2 Tbsp
Garlic	1 clove, peeled

METHOD
- Drizzle French loaf slices with a little olive oil and rub with garlic clove. Grill or toast until lightly browned. Spoon generously with different toppings and garnishes.

Tomato and Herb Topping

INGREDIENTS

Sun-dried tomatoes	300 g
Onion	1, medium, peeled and chopped
Shredded fresh basil	¼ cup
Olive oil	1 Tbsp
Salt	¼ tsp
Freshly ground black pepper	1 tsp + extra to taste
Tomato sauce	125 ml
Fresh basil	for garnishing

METHOD
- Combine all ingredients except for tomato sauce and fresh basil in a bowl. Mix well.
- Top french loaf slices with a generous layer of tomato sauce.
- Spoon a generous amount of the combined ingredients on top.
- Season with extra pepper and grill for a few minutes until tomato is warmed right through. Garnish with fresh basil.
- If desired, top with herrings, olives, salmon, pepperoni, roast lamb, roast beef, grilled prawns and mushrooms.

Spicy Mango and Aubergine Topping

INGREDIENTS

Olive oil	2 Tbsp
Onion	1, medium, peeled and chopped
Garlic	1 clove, peeled and chopped
Aubergine (eggplant/brinjal)	300 g, cubed
Curry powder	1 tsp
Cumin powder	1 tsp
Salt	½ tsp
Freshly ground black pepper	1 tsp
Tomato	1, medium, cubed
Mango	1, firm and ripe, peeled and cubed
Green chilli	1, seeded and cubed
Plain yoghurt or Ricotta cheese	125 ml
Shredded coriander leaves	

METHOD
- Heat oil in a pan and sauté onion, garlic and aubergine cubes. Sprinkle curry and cumin powder. Stir for few seconds. Season with salt and pepper.
- Add tomato, mango and green chilli. Stir and remove from pan; cool.
- Combine yoghurt with coriander leaves. Spoon a generous amount onto toasts. Top with mango and aubergine mixture. Sprinkle with extra coriander leaves.

Roast Lamb and Mint Topping

INGREDIENTS

Lamb fillets	150 g
Freshly ground black pepper	to taste
Salt	to taste
Chilli powder	to taste
Olive oil	to taste
Yoghurt	to taste
Lemon juice	to taste
Sugar	to taste
Garlic	to taste
Fresh mint	to taste

METHOD
- Toss lamb in pepper, salt and chilli powder.
- Heat oil in pan and add lamb. Cook until browned all over and tender; cool.
- Combine yoghurt, lemon juice, sugar, garlic and mint in a bowl.
- Top thinly sliced lamb on toasts. Spoon a generous layer of yoghurt mixture on top.
- Garnish with desired slices of fruits - kiwi fruit, peach or mango.

Chef's Note:
- *The bread slices or toast can be prepared in advance. All toppings can be prepared a day in advance and kept refrigerated. Fresh herbs should be freshly shredded and added to toppings just before serving.*
- *Bruschettas should be assembled within 30 minutes of serving. Use a variety of toppings of your choice.*

Preparation time: 15 minutes Cooking time: 10 minutes Serves 6–8

EGG ROSETTES

INGREDIENTS

Hardboiled eggs	8, halved
Butter	1 tsp
Mayonnaise	1 Tbsp
Curry powder	1 tsp
Finely shredded parsley	1 Tbsp + extra for garnishing
Salt	¼ tsp
Freshly ground black pepper	¼ tsp
Chilli sauce	1 tsp (optional)

METHOD
- Scoop out yolks from eggs and mash yolks in bowl with butter, mayonnaise, curry powder, parsley, salt and pepper. Taste mixture and adjust seasoning if necessary.
- Place mixture in piping bag attached with a star nozzle.
- Pipe rosettes onto egg whites. Top with extra parsley.

Chef's Note:
- *Fresh herbs, cheese or pepperoni and any other desired ingredients can be added to the above mixture for variety.*
- *Instead of piping, mixture can also be spooned onto egg whites.*

From top: Egg Rosettes; Bruschetta with Toppings

Preparation time: 30 minutes Cooking time: 15 minutes Serves 4–6

CRAB CLAWS

INGREDIENTS

Frozen crab claws	12, steamed and shelled
Prawns (shrimps)	300 g, shelled and minced
Salt	1 tsp
Cold water	6 Tbsp
Freshly ground black pepper	1/4 tsp
Cornflour (cornstarch)	1 1/2 tsp
Egg	1, lightly beaten
Breadcrumbs	4 Tbsp, mixed with 4 Tbsp sesame seeds
Cooking oil	500 ml

METHOD

- Remove flesh from crab claws; keep claws. Flake flesh into tiny bits.
- In a mixing bowl, mix minced prawns with salt, iced water, pepper and cornflour. Add in crab flesh and mix well to combine. Divide into 12 portions.
- Stuff each portion into crab claw and pat into shape.
- Dip in beaten egg and coat with breadcrumbs.
- Heat oil until hot and deep-fry crab claws until golden brown. Serve with a spicy chilli sauce.

Chef's Note:
- *Fish fillets can be used instead of prawns.*
- *Crab claws can be prepared in advance and deep-fried before serving.*

Preparation time: 20 minutes Cooking time: 15 minutes Serves 4–6

SEAFOOD NIBBLES WITH CHILLI DIP

INGREDIENTS

Prawns (shrimps)	10–12, small, shelled and deveined
Squid	10–12, small, cut into 4–5-cm long pieces

BATTER

Egg yolks	3
Water	180 ml
Plain (all-purpose) flour	250 g
Salt	1 tsp
Curry powder	1 tsp
Chilli powder	1 tsp
Cooking oil for deep-frying	

CHILLI DIP

Sour cream	150 ml
Thousand Island dressing	150 ml
Salt and pepper	to taste
Chilli powder	1 tsp

METHOD

- Skewer prawns onto bamboo skewers. Score squid pieces on the inside, lengthwise and crosswise. Set aside.
- Mix together the egg yolks, water, flour, salt, curry powder and chilli powder into a batter.
- Heat oil in a pan, dip seafood in batter and fry until golden brown. Drain excess oil with paper towels.
- Prepare chilli dip. Mix all dip ingredients together.
- Serve seafood nibbles with chilli dip.

Chef's Note:
- *You may use other types of seafood if desired.*
- *You may serve this with other sauces and dips too. Yoghurt can also be used to replace the mayonnaise.*

From top: Seafood Nibbles with Chilli Dip; Crab Claws

Preparation time: 20 minutes   Serves 6–8

SUPERB SALMON DIP

INGREDIENTS

Pink salmon	1 can (210 g)
Lemon juice	2–3 Tbsp
Cream cheese	250 g
Freshly ground black pepper	1 tsp
Ground white pepper	1 tsp
Chilli flakes	1 tsp
Diced celery	2 Tbsp
Shallots	2, peeled and finely chopped

METHOD

- Drain salmon and remove skin and bones. Add lemon juice to salmon and mix together lightly.
- In a separate bowl, soften and beat cream cheese until smooth.
- Add in salmon, black and white pepper, chilli flakes, celery and shallots. Mix well to combine.
- Serve with crackers, vegetable sticks and fruit slices.

Chef's note:

- *If you prefer a smoother dip, put mixture through a food processor.*

Preparation time: 20 minutes   Cooking time: 30–35 minutes   Serves 6–8

TIRAMISU CREAM PROFITEROLES

INGREDIENTS

Butter	30 g
Water	125 ml
Salt	1/8 tsp
Vanilla essence	1 tsp
Plain (all-purpose) flour	80 g, sifted
Icing (confectioners') sugar	1 tsp
Eggs	2, about 60 g each, lightly beaten

FILLING

Whipping cream	125 ml
Mascarpone cheese	125 ml
Coffee liqueur	60 ml

TOPPING

Cooking chocolate	125 g
Butter	60 g

METHOD

- Combine butter, water, salt and vanilla essence in a pan. Bring to the boil, stirring until butter melts. Bring mixture to full rolling boil then add in sifted flour together with icing sugar all at once.
- Stir vigorously with a wooden spoon until mixture leaves the sides of the pan and forms a smooth ball.
- Remove from heat. Allow to cool slightly.
- Using an electric mixer, add beaten eggs a little at a time, beating well after each addition.
- Put heaped teaspoons of batter on lightly greased oven trays. Allow room for spreading.
- Bake in a preheated oven at 200°C for 25 minutes or until crisp.
- Prepare filling. Whip cream, then add in mascarpone cheese and coffee liqueur.
- Prepare topping. Melt chocolate and butter over a bowl of simmering water.
- Cut puffs in halves, remove any soft centre and allow to cool. When ready to serve, spoon mascarpone cream into puffs. Transfer topping to a piping bag with a plain nozzle and pipe over profiteroles.

From left: Superb Salmon Dip; Tiramisu Cream Profiteroles

Preparation time: 20 minutes   Cooking time: 15 minutes   Serves 8–12

BEEF, ASPARAGUS AND CAPSICUM ROLLS

INGREDIENTS

Beef fillet	350 g
Worcestershire sauce	3 tsp
Mustard seeds	3 tsp
Asparagus	1 bundle, about 12 pieces
Red capsicum (bell pepper)	1, sliced into sticks
Papaya	1, small, slightly green, skinned and cut into sticks
Olive oil	1 Tbsp, optional

CUCUMBER DIP

Cucumber	1, small, skinned and seeded
Onion	1, small, peeled
Yoghurt	4 Tbsp
Lemon juice	½ Tbsp
Salt	½ tsp
Roughly chopped mint leaves	1 Tbsp

METHOD

- Have beef fillet partially frozen. It is easier to slice very thin slices of beef if it is partially frozen. Cut into thin slices. Marinate with Worcestershire sauce and mustard seeds. Leave for a few hours.
- Blanch the asparagus and capsicum sticks and set aside.
- To assemble, wrap a piece of the sliced beef fillet around pieces of vegetables and papaya. Secure with a toothpick. Repeat process.
- Just before serving, heat oil in a pan and cook rolls until well browned.
- Prepare cucumber dip. Cut cucumber into cubes, place all the ingredients (except the mint) in a blender and process until smooth. Fold in the chopped mint. Season to taste.
- Serve with a sprinkling of chilli flakes or with cucumber dip.

Chef's Note:
- Rolls can be prepared a day ahead.
- You can season the beef fillet with your favourite marinades.

Preparation time: 20 minutes   Cooking time: 15 minutes   Serves 6–8

SAVOURY PEPPERONI SQUARES

INGREDIENTS

Eggs	2
Melted butter	125 ml
Courgettes (zucchini)	2, small, grated
Carrot	1, grated
Onion	1, medium, peeled and chopped
Pecans	100 g, chopped
Cheddar cheese	100 g, grated
Self-raising flour	150 g
Semolina	50 g
Pepperoni	150 g, diced
Salt and pepper	to taste

METHOD

- Heat oven to 170°C. Beat eggs and add melted butter. Mix well. Add remaining ingredients and mix until just combined. Place in a lightly greased baking pan measuring 26 x 21-cm and bake for about 20–25 minutes. When cold, cut into desired shapes and decorate as desired.

From top: Savoury Pepperoni Squares; Beef, Asparagus and Capsicum Rolls

Preparation time: 15 minutes   Serves 4–6

JAPANESE BEAN CURD WITH SAMBAL PRAWNS

INGREDIENTS

Silken soft bean curd (*tofu*)	1 tube

SAMBAL PRAWN

Cooking oil	4 Tbsp
Dried prawns (shrimps)	4 Tbsp, washed, soaked and ground
Shallots	8–10, peeled and ground
Dried chillies	6–8
Prawn (shrimp) paste	1-cm piece
Tamarind juice	1 Tbsp
Salt and sugar	to taste

METHOD
- Cut bean curd into 1-cm thick slices and steam.
- Gently lift onto Chinese spoons. Set aside to cool.
- Heat oil in a wok and fry the ground ingredients until golden brown.
- Season to taste with tamarind juice, salt and sugar.
- When ready to serve, place onto bean curd slices and garnish as desired.

Chef's Note:
- For variety, you may use any other toppings as desired—salsa, pates or sauces.

Preparation time: 20 minutes Cooking time: 20 minutes Serves 8–10

ALMOND PETIT FOURS

INGREDIENTS

Butter	185 g
Castor sugar	65 g
Marzipan*	60 g
Egg yolks	2
Plain (all-purpose) flour	220 g, sifted
Rum	1 Tbsp
Vanilla essence	1 tsp
Icing (confectioners') sugar	
Jam	

METHOD

- Cream butter and sugar together until light and fluffy. Set aside.
- Mix marzipan and egg yolks together until smooth. Gradually add to butter mixture, beating continuously. Add sifted flour. Mix well.
- Put mixture in a piping bag fitted with a fluted nozzle. Pipe mixture into little cupcake cases.
- Bake in a preheated oven at 180°C for 15–20 minutes. Cool on a wire rack.
- When cooled, sprinkle with sifted icing sugar and spoon a little jam onto the centre of each cupcake.

Chef's Note:

- You can make your own marzipan* if it is not available.

*MARZIPAN

Ground almonds	250 g
Castor sugar	250 g
Icing (confectioners') sugar	250 g
Egg yolks	2–3
Glucose	60 g

METHOD

- Mix all the ingredients together into a pliable paste.

Preparation time: 25 minutes   Serves 6–8

TURKEY FRUIT STICKS
INGREDIENTS
Smoked turkey slices	350 g
Cream cheese	250 g
Orange marmalade	1 Tbsp
Crystallised ginger	2 Tbsp
Pineapple cubes	2 Tbsp, chopped
Sesame seeds	200 g, toasted
Rock melon	½
Honeydew melon	½
Cocktail sticks	

METHOD
- Process smoked turkey slices until fine. Add cream cheese, marmalade, ginger and pineapple cubes; process until fine.
- Transfer to a bowl, cover and refrigerate for 1 hour or until firm.
- Shape 1½ level tsp of mixture into balls, toss in sesame seeds and place on a serving tray. Using a melon baller, scoop balls from rock melon and honeydew melon.
- Just before serving, thread cheesy turkey balls and melon balls onto cocktail sticks.

Chef's Note:
- This recipe can be prepared a day in advance.
- An excellent entrée for cocktails.

Preparation time: 30 minutes   Serves 6–8

FRUITY KEBABS
INGREDIENTS
Strawberries	250 g, halved
Bananas	2–3, peeled
Lemon juice	2 Tbsp
Desiccated coconut	30 g
Kiwi fruit	4, skinned and cut into wedges
Chocolate	190 ml, broken into small pieces and melted
Bamboo skewers	

METHOD
- Dip strawberry halves in melted chocolate. Allow chocolate to set.
- Dip bananas in lemon juice. Coat with coconut and press coconut down firmly. Cut into 1.5-cm thick slices.
- Thread kiwi fruit wedges, strawberry halves and banana slices onto bamboo skewers.

Chef's Note:
- Fruity kebabs can be made 3 hours in advance. You can use any other fruits too for variety.

From left: Turkey Fruit Sticks, Fruity Kebabs

Preparation time: 20 minutes   Cooking time: 30 minutes   Serves 8–10

WICKED BROWNIES

INGREDIENTS

Dark chocolate	125 g, roughly chopped
Unsalted butter	125 g, cubed
Vanilla essence	1 tsp
Eggs	2
Castor sugar	220 g
Plain (all-purpose) flour	125 g
Baking powder	1/4 tsp
Walnuts	150 g

CHOCOLATE TOPPING

Dark chocolate	200 g, broken into small pieces and melted
Butter	45 g, melted

METHOD

- Melt chocolate and butter in a bowl over a saucepan of simmering water, taking care not to boil. Remove from heat and stir in vanilla essence.
- Beat eggs and sugar together until thick and creamy. Fold into chocolate mixture. Sift flour and baking powder over chocolate mixture. Sprinkle walnuts over chocolate mixture then fold in using a spatula.
- Spoon into a greased and lined 20-cm square shallow cake tin. Smooth top using a spatula. Bake in a preheated oven at 180°C for 20–25 minutes or until just set. Cool in pan on a wire rack.
- To make topping, combine chocolate and butter in a mixing bowl until well blended. Spread over brownie and set aside to firm.
- Cut into neat squares to serve.

Chef's Note:
- *Use almond flakes if walnuts are not available.*

Preparation time: 15 minutes   Cooking time: 15 minutes   Serves 4–6

PRAWN EGG ROLLS

INGREDIENTS

Prawns (shrimps)	350 g, shelled and minced
Spring onions (scallions)	2 sprigs, chopped
Green chilli	1, chopped
Red chilli	1, chopped
Mushrooms	2, chopped
Ground white pepper	1 tsp
Salt	1 tsp
Sugar	1 tsp
Cornflour (cornstarch)	1 tsp
Butter	60 g
Eggs	4, lightly beaten

METHOD

- In a bowl, combine all the ingredients except for butter and eggs. Set aside.
- To make omelette, whip eggs and season with a pinch of salt and pepper.
- Brush a non-stick pan with a little butter and pour half the amount of beaten eggs in and swirl to make a perfect omelette. Allow to cook and set aside; repeat process to make another omelette.
- Place both omelettes on a flat surface.
- Spread prawn mixture onto the omelettes and roll up neatly. Steam for 8–10 minutes. When done, cut into neat slices and serve with a chilli sauce.

Chef's Note:
- *Prawns can be replaced by fish or using a combination of both prawns and fish is just as delicious.*

Preparation time: 30 minutes Cooking time: 20 minutes Serves 6–8

TOMATO CHEESE TARTLETS

INGREDIENTS

PASTRY
Wholemeal flour	75 g
Plain (all-purpose) flour	75 g
Paprika	1 tsp
Butter	30 g
Freshly grated Parmesan cheese	50 g + extra for sprinkling
Water	2–3 Tbsp

FILLING
Olive oil	1 Tbsp
Shallots	3, small, peeled and cubed
Garlic	2 cloves, peeled and cubed
Courgette (zucchini)	1, small, cubed
Semi-dried tomatoes	50 g, cubed
Pitted chopped black olives	50 g
Basil leaves	2 Tbsp
Freshly ground black pepper	1 tsp

METHOD

PASTRY
- Sift dry ingredients into a bowl, rub in butter, stir in grated cheese and enough water to make into a soft dough.
- Knead on a floured surface until dough is smooth; refrigerate covered for 30 minutes.
- Roll out dough to 2-mm thickness. Cut out rounds from dough with a 9-cm round pastry cutter.
- Place rounds in 7-cm tart pans, prick pastry all over with fork. Bake in a moderate oven for about 15 minutes or until lightly browned; leave to cool.
- Just before serving, spoon filling into pastry cases, sprinkle with flaked Parmesan cheese.

- Prepare filling. Heat oil in pan and add shallots, garlic and courgette. Cook, stirring, for about 30 minutes or until shallots are soft; remove from heat, stir in tomatoes, olives and basil leaves.
- Sprinkle ground black pepper and sprinkle with freshly grated Parmesan cheese.

Chef's Note:
- Pastry can be prepared a day or two earlier. If there's no time in preparing short crust pastry, buy ready rolled sheets.

Preparation time: 15 minutes Serves 4–6

OLIVE AND SMOKED TURKEY SQUARES

INGREDIENTS
Cream cheese	25 g
Freshly ground black pepper	½ tsp
White bread	6 slices
Brown bread	3 slices
Smoked turkey slices	150 g
Avocado	1, skinned and mashed
Kiwi fruit	2, skinned and sliced
Strawberries	15, halved
Pitted olives	15, halved
Toothpicks	27

METHOD
- Beat cream cheese and coarsely ground black peppercorns in a bowl until smooth.
- Spread 3 bread slices with some cheese mixture, top with a layer of turkey, then spread thinly with avocado.
- Spread another 3 slices of bread with cheese mixture, place cheese side down on previous slices.
- Repeat spreading and layering with remaining cheese mixture, turkey, avocado and bread.
- Trim crusts from sandwiches; cut each sandwich into 3 fingers then cut each finger into 3 cubes. Using toothpicks, skewer a slice of kiwi fruit, a strawberry half and an olive onto each cube.

Chef's Note:
- Bread cubes can be made 2–3 hours in advance. Make sure to cover bread cubes with a damp cloth or cling film.

From top: Tomato Cheese Tartlets; Olive and Smoked Turkey Squares

75

Preparation time: 15 minutes   Cooking time: 20 minutes   Serves 4–6

SPICY HERB POTATO WEDGES

INGREDIENTS

Potatoes	4, large, each cut into 8 wedges
Butter	1 Tbsp, melted
Olive oil	2 Tbsp
Garlic	1 clove, peeled and finely chopped
Oregano	1 Tbsp
Rosemary	1 Tbsp
Chilli powder	1 tsp
Freshly ground black peppercorn	1 tsp
Freshly grated Parmesan cheese	30 g
Coarse sea salt	1 tsp

SOUR CREAM DIP

Sour cream	250 ml
Black peppercorns	1 tsp

METHOD

- Preheat oven at 200°C.
- In a mixing bowl, combine butter, olive oil, garlic, oregano, rosemary, chilli powder and black peppercorn.
- Add in potatoes and toss gently to coat with the mixture completely.
- Place potatoes on an oven tray in a single layer and bake for 25–30 minutes.
- Turn wedges on their sides and sprinkle with Parmesan cheese.
- Prepare sour cream dip. Mix together sour cream and black peppercorns. Serve with potato wedges.
- Bake for a further 10–15 minutes. Sprinkle coarse sea salt. Serve hot with sour cream dip.

Chef's Note:
- Best prepared close to serving.

Preparation time: 20 minutes   Cooking time: 15 minutes   Serves 4–6

SPICY CHICKEN NIBBLES

INGREDIENTS

Chicken thigh fillets	700 g, cut into 8–10 pieces
Plain yoghurt	125 ml
Tandoori paste*	125 ml
Curry powder	1 tsp
Spring onions (scallions)	2 sprigs, cut into 2-cm lengths
Toothpicks	

YOGHURT DIP

Yoghurt	60 g
Mayonnaise	60 g
Curry powder	1 tsp
Lemon juice	1 tsp

METHOD

- Marinate chicken with yoghurt, tandoori paste and curry powder for 3 hours or overnight.
- To make spring onion frills, make fine cuts close together halfway down each 2-cm length.
- Just before serving, cook undrained chicken pieces in batches on heated greased griddle pan or grill until browned all over and tender.
- Prepare yoghurt dip. Mix all dip ingredients together.
- Serve chicken pieces on toothpicks. Garnish with spring onion frills and yoghurt dip.

Chef's Note:
- Fish or prawns can be used instead of chicken.
- Better flavour is achieved when marinated overnight.
- If tandoori paste is not available, make your own and refrigerate.

*TANDOORI PASTE

Yoghurt	250 ml
Tomato purée	125 ml
Ground coriander	1 Tbsp
Chilli powder	1 Tbsp
Ground mustard	1 Tbsp
Sugar	1 tsp
Salt	1 tsp
Onion	1, large, peeled and grated
Garlic	3 cloves, peeled and grated

METHOD

- Combine all ingredients in a jar and mix well. Keep refrigerated and use within a week.

From top: Spicy Herb Potato Wedges; Spicy Chicken Nibbles

Preparation time: 15 minutes   Cooking time: 5 minutes   Chilling time: 1 hour

A TRAY OF TRUFFLES

INGREDIENTS

Plain chocolate	150 g, broken into small pieces
Butter cake	125 g, broken into crumbs
Icing (confectioners') sugar	1 Tbsp
Ground almonds	100 g
Brandy	2 Tbsp (optional)
Double cream	80 ml
Cocoa powder	60 g

METHOD

- Melt chocolate in a bowl over simmering water. Set aside.
- In another bowl, combine butter cake crumbs, icing sugar, almonds and brandy. Gradually pour melted chocolate into mixture and mix well. Pour in double cream to bind mixture together. Refrigerate mixture for at least 1 hour.
- Take a 1 tsp of mixture and roll into a ball. Decide which fillings or coatings you want.

CHOOSE A FILLING

LIQUOR TRUFFLES
- Replace brandy with 2 Tbsp of your favorite liqueur - Grand Marnier, Rum or Tia Maria are all delicious.
- Omit brandy. Soak 75 g raisins in 4 tsp of rum for a couple of hours and add to the basic mixture.

WHITE CHOCOLATE
- Replace plain chocolate with white chocolate and use clear alcohol such as Malibu or Cointreau.

CHOOSE A COATING

PLAIN CHOCOLATE
- Melt 125 g chocolate in a bowl over pan of simmering water. Using a skewer, dip truffles into melted chocolate.

CHOCOLATE VERMICELLI
- Sprinkle 50 g of chocolate vermicelli on a plate and roll truffles in it to form a thick, even coating.

COCONUT COATING
- Sprinkle 50 g of desiccated coconut on a plate and roll truffles in coconut until they are evenly coated with a thick layer.

- Sift cocoa powder onto a sheet of greaseproof paper. Roll balls in it until lightly coated. Shake gently to get rid of excess cocoa powder.
- Refrigerate for 2 hours until set.
- Serve, placed in little cup cases.

Chef's Note:
- *When choosing a plain chocolate coating, use a plain nozzle on piping bag and drizzle different designs on truffles. Using one basic recipe and a few extra ingredients, you can make a brilliant selection of homemade truffles.*

Preparation time: 20 minutes Serves 4–6

CUCUMBER SLICES WITH CHEESE TOPPING

INGREDIENTS

Cream cheese	125 g
Sour cream	1 Tbsp
Basil	1 Tbsp, chopped
Parsley	1 Tbsp, chopped
Oregano	1 tsp + extra for garnishing
Rosemary	½ tsp
Shallots	2, peeled, shredded and sliced
Lemon juice	1 tsp
Cucumber	1, sliced into 2 cm slices
Black pitted olives	10
Red capsicum (bell pepper)	½, sliced

METHOD

- Blend cream cheese, sour cream, herbs, shallots and lemon juice until smooth.
- Top cucumber slices with cream cheese mixture, then extra oregano, olives and red capsicum slices.
- Cover refrigerated for 2 hours.

Chef's Note:

- An excellent dish that is easy to prepare. Sprinkle some beef bacon cubes on top. For a more spicy flavour, sprinkle some coarsely ground black pepper.

Glossary

Avocadoes
Avocadoes are very nutritious for the body and the skin. They contain a nutritious natural fat that lowers the cholesterol level in the blood and they contain a lot of vitamin A, B and E. Avocado is used in a lot of skincare products.

Honeydews
Honeydews are large, round fruits with smooth, greenish ivory skin and sweet, juicy, light green flesh. Keep them at room temperature or in the sun depending on how soon you want them to ripen. If they are ripe, store them in the refrigerator.

Mangoes
Mangoes are oval-shaped tropical fruits with very juicy, aromatic orange flesh and yellow skin tinged with orange when ripe. Ripen firm mangoes at room temperature in an open paper or plastic bag.

Bananas
There are many varieties of bananas available. To stop discolouration after peeling, toss them in lemon juice.

Kiwi Fruits
These are brown, slightly hairy fruits with a thin skin covering a tender green flesh with a ring of fine, dark seeds in the middle. The sweet sour taste is delicate and refreshing. Also known as Chinese gooseberries, they are versatile and can be used in salads, cheesecakes, garnishes, sherbets, mousses, starters, pavlovas, chutneys and relishes.

Choux Pastry
A moist dough of flour, butter, eggs and water is piped into various shapes and baked. The resulting pastry is used to prepare desserts such as cream puffs, eclairs and profiteroles.

Glacé Cherries
These small, round red to black fruits are botanically designated drupes, or stone fruits. Usually available in jars.

Oranges
There are many varieties available all year round. They are mainly eaten raw. Their strong flavour is used in both sweet and savoury dishes.

Potatoes
Potatoes are available in hundreds of varieties including russet, long white, red, Yukon gold and yellow fin. Specific varieties, such as russet, are best for baking and frying whereas others, such as red potatoes, are best for boiling. Choose potatoes that are firm with tight unblemished skin, having no sprouts or green areas. Store in a cool dark area. Do not refrigerate, as the cold temperature will convert the starches into sugars, creating a measly, dark potato. To prevent darkening, toss sliced, uncooked potatoes in a mixture of 250 ml water and $^1/_2$ tsp cream of tartar; drain and proceed with recipe.

Sweet Potatoes (Kumara)
Sweet potatoes are tubers with light to deep red skin and pale yellow to orange flesh that is sweet when cooked. Pick sweet potatoes with firm, smooth skin. Store in a cool, dark place and use within 1 week.

Pineapples
Pineapples are very juicy when ripe and are used in fruit salad, flans, hot puddings, cakes, meat and fish dishes, jam pickles and drinks. Also called Ananas, they are far better eaten fresh than cooked. It has a tenderizing effect on meat similar to that of papaya.

Strawberries
Which are at their peak from spring to midsummer, are plump, red, juicy, and intensely sweet when ripe. Select unbruised, slightly soft berries with a deep colour and an inviting fragrance. Store unwashed and loosely covered in a single layer on a tray or platter lined with paper towels in the refrigerator for a few days. Substitute berries frozen without syrup when fresh are not available.

Tomatoes
Categorised botanically as fruits, they are eaten as a vegetable and enjoyed for their combination of sweetness and acidity. Fresh varieties are available all year. Colours vary from red to yellow to green and purple and shapes from the bulky beefsteak and the large common tomato to the small cherry tomato. Tomatoes are sold fresh or in cans.

Glossary

Cheddar Cheese
A firm, smooth-textured, whole-milk cheese, that ranges in colour from pale yellow-white to deep yellow-orange and in taste from mild and sweet when fresh to sharp and tangy when aged.

Cottage Cheese
Cottage cheese is a fresh cheese made from whole, part-skimmed or skimmed pasteurised cow's milk. It has a mild, bland flavour and is quite moist.

Mozzarella Cheese
Mozzarella cheese is a rindless white, mild-tasting Italian variety of cheese traditionally made from water buffalo's milk. Commercially produced cow's milk Mozzarella is much more common, but less flavourful.

Choux Pastry
A moist dough of flour, butter, eggs and water is piped into various shapes and baked. The resulting pastry is used to prepare desserts such as cream puffs, eclairs and profiteroles.

Mayonnaise
Mayonnaise is a rich, creamy dressing made with egg yolks, vegetable oil, mustard and vinegar or lemon juice. It has multiple uses as a condiment, as a seasoning ingredient and as a thickener.

Parmesan Cheese
A hard, thick-crusted Italian cow's milk cheese. It has a sharp, salty, full flavour resulting from up to 2 years of aging. It takes its name from the city of Parma, though it originated midway between that city and Reggio, where the finest Italian variety, Parmigiano-Reggiano, is produced. Buy in block form to grate fresh as needed.

Wasabi
Wasabi is a condiment traditionally served with raw fish and soba dishes in Japan. The ground root-like rhizome pungently flavours many foods in Japanese cuisine and its bright green colour adds contrast. Used as an ingredient in dressings, dips, sauces and marinades, this versatile spice is rapidly becoming one of the most popular new flavours in Western cuisine. It has a heat component that unlike chillies is not long-lived on the palate and subsides into an extremely pleasant, mild vegetable taste.

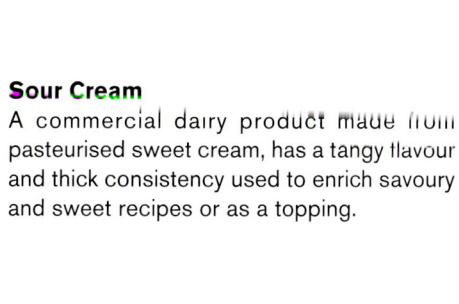

Sour Cream
A commercial dairy product made from pasteurised sweet cream, has a tangy flavour and thick consistency used to enrich savoury and sweet recipes or as a topping.

Yoghurt
Yoghurt is milk fermented by bacterial cultures that impart a mildly acidic flavour and custard-like texture. So-called plain yoghurt refers to the unflavoured product. Plain and flavoured yoghurts are available made from whole, low-fat or non-fat milk. Use the plain type for the recipes.

WEIGHTS & MEASURES

LIQUID AND VOLUME MEASURES

Metric	Imperial	American
5 ml	1/6 fl oz	1 teaspoon
10 ml	1/3 fl oz	1 dessertspoon
15 ml	1/2 fl oz	1 tablespoon
60 ml	2 fl oz	1/4 cup (4 tablespoons)
85 ml	2 1/2 fl oz	1/3 cup
90 ml	3 fl oz	3/8 cup (6 tablespoons)
125 ml	4 fl oz	1/2 cup
180 ml	6 fl oz	3/4 cup
250 ml	8 fl oz	1 cup
300 ml	10 fl oz (1/2 pint)	1 1/4 cups
375 ml	12 fl oz	1 1/2 cups
435 ml	14 fl oz	1 3/4 cups
500 ml	16 fl oz	2 cups
625 ml	20 fl oz (1 pint)	2 1/2 cups
750 ml	24 fl oz (1 1/5 pints)	3 cups
1 litre	32 fl oz (1 3/5 pints)	4 cups
1.25 litres	40 fl oz (2 pints)	5 cups
1.5 litres	48 fl oz (2 2/5 pints)	6 cups
2.5 litres	80 fl oz (4 pints)	10 cups

LENGTH

Metric	Imperial
0.5 cm	1/4 inch
1 cm	1/2 inch
1.5 cm	3/4 inch
2.5 cm	1 inch

ABBREVIATION

tsp	teaspoon
Tbsp	tablespoon
g	gram
kg	kilogram
ml	millilitre

DRY MEASURES

Metric	Imperial
30 grams	1 ounce
45 grams	1 1/2 ounces
55 grams	2 ounces
70 grams	2 1/2 ounces
85 grams	3 ounces
100 grams	3 1/2 ounces
110 grams	4 ounces
125 grams	4 1/2 ounces
140 grams	5 ounces
280 grams	10 ounces
450 grams	16 ounces (1 pound)
500 grams	1 pound, 1 1/2 ounces
700 grams	1 1/2 pounds
800 grams	1 3/4 pounds
1 kilogram	2 pounds, 3 ounces
1.5 kilograms	3 pounds, 4 1/2 ounces
2 kilograms	4 pounds, 6 ounces

OVEN TEMPERATURE

	°C	°F	Gas Regulo
Very slow	120	250	1
Slow	150	300	2
Moderately slow	160	325	3
Moderate	180	350	4
Moderately hot	190/200	370/400	5/6
Hot	210/220	410/440	6/7
Very hot	230	450	8
Super hot	250/290	475/550	9/10